Representation, Inclusion, and Innovation

Multidisciplinary Explorations

Synthesis Lectures on Human-Centered Informatics

Editor
John M. Carroll, *Penn State University*

Human-Centered Informatics (HCI) is the intersection of the cultural, the social, the cognitive, and the aesthetic with computing and information technology. It encompasses a huge range of issues, theories, technologies, designs, tools, environments, and human experiences in knowledge work, recreation and leisure activity, teaching and learning, and the potpourri of everyday life. The series publishes state-of-the-art syntheses, case studies, and tutorials in key areas. It shares the focus of leading international conferences in HCI.

Common Ground in Electronically Mediated Conversation

Andrew Monk

2008

Representation, Inclusion, and Innovation: Multidisciplinary Explorations
Clayton Lewis

ISBN: 978-3-031-01093-4 print
ISBN: 978-3-031-02221-0 ebook
ISBN: 978-3-031-00201-4 hardcover

DOI 10.1007/978-3-031-02221-0

A Publication in the Springer series
SYNTHESIS LECTURES ON HUMAN-CENTERED INFORMATICS, #38
Series Editors: John M. Carroll, Penn State University

Series ISSN: 1946-7680 Print   1946-7699 Electronic

Representation, Inclusion, and Innovation

Multidisciplinary Explorations

Clayton Lewis

University of Colorado, Boulder

SYNTHESIS LECTURES ON HUMAN-CENTERED INFORMATICS #38

ABSTRACT

A representation is a thing that can be interpreted as providing information about something: a map, or a graph, for example. This book is about the expanding world of computational representations, representations that use the power of computation to provide information in new forms, and in new ways. Unlike printed maps or graphs, computational representations can be dynamic, and even interactive, so that what is represented, and how, can be shaped by user actions. Exploring these new possibilities can be guided by an emerging theory of representation, that clarifies what characteristics representations must have to express the meaning being represented, and to enable users to discern that meaning easily and accurately. The theory also shows the way to inclusive design, for example using sounds to represent information commonly presented visually, so that people who cannot see can understand what is being presented. Because representations must be shaped by the abilities of their users, and by the nature of the meanings they convey, creating them requires perspectives from multiple disciplines, including psychology, as well as computer science, and the sciences appropriate to the content being expressed. The book presents a series of explorations of this large and complicated space, as invitations to further study, and to innovation.

KEYWORDS

representations, inclusive design, visualization, interactive simulations, aesthetics, visual programming

Contents

Preface

What characterizes … new media are their unprecedented dynamics, based on their underlying computational mechanisms. …[W]e need the creative elaboration of the particular dynamic capabilities that these new media afford and of the ways that through them humans and machines together can perform interesting new effects. These are avenues that have just begun to be explored, primarily in the fields of new media, graphics and animation, art and design. Not only do these experiments promise innovations in our thinking about machines, but they also open up the equally exciting prospect of new conceptualizations of what it means to be human, understood not as a bounded, rational entity, but as an unfolding, shifting biography of culturally specific experience and relations, inflected for each of us in uniquely particular ways.

–Suchman (2007), p. 23.

Representations are all around us: a map represents a place, a picture can represent a person, a curve drawn on paper can represent a mathematical function, this book represents a collection of ideas. We'll get more technical about just what representations are, and how they work, but for now we'll use examples like these to suggest that a representation is a thing that can be interpreted as providing information *about* something, that is, about whatever is being represented.

The human world has always been full of representations, as far back as we can see, but it's never been fuller than now. That's because of *computation*, whose power is highlighted by Lucy Suchman in the quotation above. The reason computation is so useful, in almost everything that people do, is because of the fabulous resources it offers for new ways of representing things, all kinds of things. These new representations have miraculous advantages over what's been available until now. At the dawn of writing a representation of a few words would be a lump of clay, of substantial size and weight; today, all the books ever published could be fit into a storage device that would fit in your hand; see http://www.gizmodo.co.uk/2016/12/every-book-ever-published-would-fit-on-to-one-hard-disk/. Further, computational representations of books can be sent to the other side of the world with virtually no delay, they can be copied with essentially no delay, and at essentially no cost, and so on.

And we aren't at all limited to representing things like the contents of books. We can create dynamic, animated presentations; what it took the Disney studios weeks to do not long ago can be done today by a schoolchild at their desk. We can create sounds, music, and synthetic speech, all computationally, meaning that these representations share the virtues of lightness, smallness, ease of transmission, and ease of replication of computationally represented text. But more than that, we can control and vary the production of any of these things very easily. A program that creates music won't produce just some particular piece of music, it will let you create the music you want (if you have the patience and skill). And you can interact with the program. It doesn't just produce whatever representation it makes, on its own; it shows you what it is doing and invites you to modify it, while production is going on. An atlas was once a collection of printed maps. If you wanted a different map you had to get a different atlas. Now you can use computational representations that allow you to shape what you want the map to show, and how, with enormous flexibility, and change the view you get as you get it, so as to focus on what you want to see, even if you didn't know what you wanted to see when you started.

> Box I.1
>
> The sociologist Bruno Latour, in his essay, "Visualization and Cognition: Thinking with Eyes and Hands" (1986), has described the profound impact of *inscriptions*, things like maps, drawings, diagrams, and tables, on the progress and practice of science. He lists nine properties of such representations that make them especially useful.
>
> They can be *moved* easily from one place to another.
>
> They *don't change* when they are moved.
>
> They are *flat*, and hence content is not hidden.
>
> Their *scale is flexible*, so that structures of very different sizes can be rendered conveniently.
>
> They can be *reproduced* cheaply.
>
> They can be *recombined*, so that information about different things can be brought together. One form of recombination is superimposition.
>
> They can be *made part of a written text*.
>
> They can be analyzed using *two-dimensional geometry*, so that (for example) the sizes of things can be readily measured.
>
> We can see that computational representations intensify some of these benefits; for example, computational representations can be moved and reproduced even more easily than inscriptions on paper, such as Latour studied. Operations like rescaling, recombination, or measurement also become easier and cheaper. But the potential of computational representations goes beyond intensifying the benefits of inscriptions to providing new ones: interactive control, moving images, the integration of sound and image, and much more.

One of the consequences of the enormous new potential of computational representations is to greatly expand the audience for information of all kinds. It used to be that blind people could only read newspapers if someone else read the material and recorded it, or transcribed it as Braille. Today, almost all newspapers provide computational representations of their content that can be presented to anyone as synthetic speech. This is an example of the potential of computational representations to support *inclusive design*, that is, the design of representations that can be processed effectively by the widest audience.

This book is about this expanding world of computational representations, including its potential for inclusive design. I'm writing it because, exciting as what we can now do every day is, there's more that we can do. I also think that the frontiers of what we can do, the new possibilities, are *interesting*, as well as important, and I want to share the excitement I feel about them.

So this book isn't meant to be a report of what I or other people have already done. Rather, it's a report of *explorations*, attempts to push back those frontiers. As you'll see, the explorations are all incomplete, and some are, so far at any rate, failures. Maybe none of them will prove to have mapped territory that people in the future will find especially useful. But I hope to show something of what's out there, and what you will see if you go there yourself. I'm hoping that you'll find more than I have.

When exploring something, it's helpful to have some kind of map, however rough, within which to sketch the new things you find. I've found it helpful to use a theory for this, a *theory of representation*, that is broad enough to encompass the wide range of content and technology with which we will be concerned. As discussed in the next chapter, this theory is built on a substantial mathematical foundation, something called the *representational theory of measurement*. It adds vital insights from the work of Jock Mackinlay, who showed how this kind of theory can expose the key challenges in creating any representation, of anything: *expressiveness*, that is, the ability for a representation to be faithful to the structure of what's being represented, and *effectiveness*, the requirement that the operations that have to be performed to use a representation, for example comparing the lengths of two bars in a bar chart, can be performed easily and accurately by whoever has to perform them. One can see that what's effective for one person won't necessarily be effective for another: someone who can't see the bars can't readily compare their lengths. This is the aspect of the theory that supports inclusive design.

As we've seen, representations today can be highly dynamic, and interactive. I sketch how the theory can be expanded to provide a useful way to think about these kinds of representations, as well as the familiar static ones that sit still on a page or on a screen.

This theory requires ideas from more than one discipline to deploy it, which is to say that ideas from more than one discipline are required to develop new representations. The theory distinguishes two domains, a *target* domain, which is whatever we are actually interested in, for example world affairs, and a *representation* domain, which contains whatever the representation itself is, for example words printed on paper, or synthetic speech. Building new representations requires ideas about both domains. For the representation domain, we may need to know about printing, or (for all the explorations reported here) computer programs, the displays they produce, and how to support possible ways of interacting with them. We also need ideas from the target domain: what is it about world affairs that we care about? What does the representation need to help us do?

The effectiveness requirement brings in even more ideas, quite different ones. If our representations are going to be consumed by people, we need to know what people can do easily, and what they can't. This is psychology. I hope you will enjoy having all these ideas, from different fields, rattling around together.

As we develop this theory we'll see how it relates to ideas that are familiar to many computer scientists and programmers, the separation of presentation from content, and design patterns that separate *models* from *views*. These ideas take advantage of a natural *layering* that appears in many representations: the representation domain for one representation becomes the target domain for another. So a system can contain a model, that represents some content of interest, but cannot directly be observed by a user; a view then represents the model in a way that the user can observe. To be useful, the view has to be effective, in Mackinlay's sense, and the composite of model and view must be expressive, that is, it must faithfully reflect the structure of the underlying content.

All the explorations in the book involve computational representations, and nearly all the chapters include computer programs that illustrate the ideas. The programs can be accessed from http://claytonhalllewis.github.io/bookPage.html. These programs are not finished work, so please don't expect them to be. I am a shocking programmer, and not at all a "software engineer;" that is, the programs are full of things no one should do. I shouldn't have done them, either, but in trying out the ideas, as they developed, I just didn't make the investment I should have to make the programs clear and clean. The programs have hardly been tested at all; as the wise Antranig Basman has suggested, such programs are "not even software." So please don't take any of the programs as exemplary as programs.

One of the many wonderful things about the world we now live in is that programs like these can be provided to you in a form that you can not only play with, but also modify, to try new ideas of your own, or to make improvements. All of them are written in Javascript, and should run for you in Chrome, Firefox, or Safari, with no need for you to install anything on your computer. Most use no code that isn't already in your browser; for the few exceptions I've included copies of the other code in what's available to you. There's nothing exotic. If you are new to Javascript, or for that matter to programming, there are excellent materials online, for example https://developer.mozilla.org/en-US/docs/Learn/Getting_started_with_the_web/JavaScript_basics, if you know how to create a web page, or https://www.w3schools.com/js/ if you do not. The latter site lets you play with the language in your browser without setting up a web page of your own.

The target domains for the representations in the explorations are varied. The explorations in Chapters 2–4 are about physics concepts. The material is drawn from a large collection of interactive simulations for learning physics developed by my colleagues at the University of Colorado, Boulder, and made available online at https://phet.colorado.edu. They key interest here is, how can one make interactive simulations like these work for people who don't see well? The target domain for Chapters 5 and 6 are programs, written in "visual languages" intended to make programming easier for beginners. Here again the challenge is, how can the conceptual benefits of these "visual languages" work for people who can't work with visual material? A popular programming activity for beginners is turtle graphics, a simple way to make a program draw pictures. Chapter 7 explores how turtle graphics might be made to use sounds rather than drawings. Many people feel that music conveys spatial movement to them as they listen. Chapter 8 explores whether this could be developed as a way to convey graphical information in sound. Chapter 9 explores how forms in more than three spatial dimensions might be represented. Such forms are easy to represent mathematically, but most people find that representation difficult to understand. Can we develop representations that are easier to understand? Finally, the target domain for the exploration in Chapter 10 is programs, again, but here the kind of programs that people in the arts sometimes use. Might it be possible to develop representations of programs that have more aesthetic potential than the textual and visual languages that we have today, and that might have other advantages, such as being more directly intelligible? I've not been able to do this, but perhaps you can.

Many people have helped with this work, by contributing ideas and suggestions, or as collaborators on some of the projects. Of course none of them is to blame for the roughness, or downright wrongness, of the ideas and the programs. They include Tamer Amin, Sina Bahram, Antranig Basman, Alan Blackwell, Beat Brogle, Bill Casson, Hunter Ewen, Michael Eisenberg, Noah Finkelstein, Inge Hinterwaldner, Varsha Koushik, Richard Ladner, Owen Lewis, Emily Moore, Steve Pollock, Alex Repenning, Derek Riemer, Ben Shapiro, Taliesin Smith, Andreas Stefik, and Jason White. Frieder Nake kindly provided examples of his work. Prof. Mehul Bhatt of the University of Bremen welcomed me into his research group. The ATLAS Institute at the University of Colorado Boulder supported some of the work. Colin Clark and an anonymous reviewer read the manuscript in draft and made many valuable suggestions.

For the programs that accompany the book I am indebted to the wonderful ecosystem of freely-available code to do all kinds of things, that the web offers us. Of special value are Blockly, a library for creating blocks languages, created by a group led by Neil Fraser of Google; Flocking, a sound processing system created by Colin Clark of OCAD University; and Raphaël, a library that makes SVG graphics much easier, provided by Dmitry Baranovskiy. The Stack Overflow community, both the people who ask questions, and those who answer them, provided enormously helpful information.

I owe more than I can express to the Hanse-Wissenschaftskolleg, in Delmenhorst, Germany, its Rector, Prof. Dr. Reto Weiler, and its wonderful staff, including Dr. Dorothe Poggel, Research Manager for the Brain area at the HWK. A six-month fellowship in residence at the HWK provided an opportunity for reading, programming, and discussion that made it possible to undertake the book. The international community of fellows, staff, and associates, including Tamer Amin, Margarita Balmaceda, Ann Blake, Jacopo Dal Corso, Marion Daniel, Susanne Fuchs, Alessa Geiger, Christina Gehrking, Petra Heinz, Stefan Heinz, Kim Hoke, Ian McDonald, Heidi Mueller-Henicz, Lucy Pao, Claire Raymond, AJ Reese, Brandi Reese, Thierry Ribault, Susanne Schregel, Amritashis Sengupta, Dipa Sengupta, Nicole Schuck, Elizabeth Sheffield, Li Shu, Wolfgang Stenzel, and Ilka Weniger provided an environment both intellectually stimulating and socially enjoyable. I thank all concerned with this wonderful institute, including the community members in the Verein der Freunde und Förderer des Hanse-Wissenschaftskollegs in Delmenhorst e.V. who do so much to support it. I also thank my colleague Gerhard Fischer, now emeritus, for decades of collaboration, and for telling me about the HWK.

The encouragement and support of Jack Carroll, Diane Cerra, Deborah Gabriel, and the Morgan & Claypool organization were essential to the project, and I am very grateful.

Finally, I thank David Krantz for including the theory of measurement in the Experimental Psychology Proseminar at the University of Michigan in the Fall of 1973.

CHAPTER 1

Theory of Representation

Informally, a representation is a thing that provides information about something else, the way a map provides information about a place. But although this definition provided a starting point for our discussion in the last chapter, we need to move beyond it. A huge problem with it is that it says that a representation is a thing, but in fact a thing, in itself, can't be a representation.

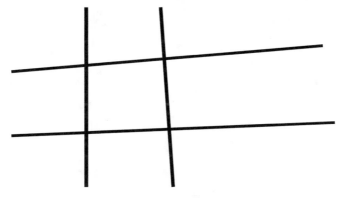

Figure 1.1: Lines in a grid, forming a tic-tac-toe board, or a map, or … .

How can this be? Aren't maps things, and aren't maps representations? Figure 1.1 brings out the trouble. Is that diagram a rough map of a portion of downtown Boulder, Colorado? Or is it a tic-tac-toe board? Or is it a rough map of a portion of lower Manhattan? As a thing, in itself, the diagram could be any of these things, or none of them… there is no way to know. Only when accompanied by some interpretation, that specifies what the diagram is a representation of, does it become a representation.

Box 1.1

Ruth Millikan and What Things Represent

The philosopher Ruth Millikan argues that things can be representations by virtue of their causal history: something can be considered a representation if the way it came into being depended on its representing something (Millikan, 1989). If when I drew the diagram in Figure 1.1 I drew what I did because I wanted a map of Boulder, then it is a map of Boulder.

More interestingly, a structure in an organism can be said to be a representation if its contribution to the evolution of the organism depends on its representational role. For example, Millikan argues that a particular structure that is sensitive to magnetic fields, in certain tiny marine organisms, actually represents the direction of oxygen-poor water. In the part of the ocean where these creatures live the earth's magnetic field aligns with gravity, which is difficult for tiny organisms to sense, "Down" is the direction of oxygen-poor water. The direction of the magnetic field, in itself, isn't important to these organisms; neither is gravity. But the direction of oxygen-poor water is important. So the structure is there because of the information it provides about oxygen-poor water, and, Millikan says, that's therefore what it represents.

Relating Millikan's thinking to our framing, can a thing in itself be a representation, for Millikan? Perhaps so: she might say that that structure represents something, and what it represents is determined by its history, whether we know the history or not. Thus, Figure 1.1 is or isn't a map of Boulder, whether we know it or not: its history, if we knew it, would answer the question.

Suppose I am discussing Manhattan, and I reach for Figure 1.1 to aid in my description. Then, in that setting, the figure would be a representation of Manhattan, because that's why I introduced it. This would be true, in that setting, even if whoever originally drew Figure 1.1 intended it to be a map of Boulder.

We'll sidestep these perplexities by not considering that the figure is a representation except when considered along with an interpretation. We won't ask whether or when the needed interpretation could be recovered from the figure's history. Rather, we'll consider that a thing like Figure 1.1 is a representation only when considered as a part of a *representational system* that provides the interpretation we need.

The representational theory of measurement (RTM; Krantz et al., 2007) provides a starting point for developing these ideas. RTM describes measurement as establishing a *structure-preserving mapping* between an empirical relational structure and a mathematical relational structure. We'll refer to these structures as the *target domain*, a domain in which we have practical interest, and the *representation domain*. The "structure preserving mapping" is the interpretation we need to tell us that something is being used as a representation, of what, and how.

Measurement of length provides a familiar example that illustrates these ideas. Suppose we are in the situation depicted in Figure 1.2, in which we need to bridge a chasm, and we have a supply of logs. We want to know whether a given log will bridge the chasm. We could do this by actual trial, but that would involve hard work, and possibly even danger, as we maneuver the log at the brink of the chasm.

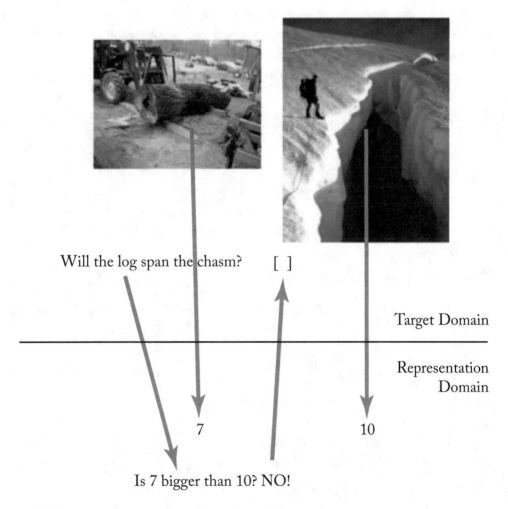

Figure 1.2: Using measurement to determine if a log will span a chasm.

Of course we realize that we can use measurement to answer this question, without moving the logs at all. We measure a log, and we measure the chasm (using a little trigonometry, if necessary), and we compare the numbers we get. If the number we get from measuring the log is bigger than the measurement of the chasm, the log is long enough; otherwise, it's not.

Now suppose none of the logs is long enough, but we have some means of joining logs end to end. Now we want to know if some combination of logs will be long enough. How can we tell how long a combination will be? Here again, we could do the physical work of connecting the logs, and then measure them. But we can avoid this work using measurement: we know that we can predict the length we can span by connecting logs end to end by *adding* the lengths of the separate logs.

These facts about measurement are an everyday miracle. How can it be that we can predict the results of physical actions, like laying a log across a chasm, or connecting logs together, by manipulating numbers? See Box 1.2 for discussion.

Box 1.2

Why does measurement work?

The physicist Eugene Wigner, in a famous essay, "The Unreasonable Effectiveness of Mathematics in the Natural Sciences" (1995; first published 1960), points out the surprisingness of the correspondence between physical phenomena and relatively simple mathematical structures. He offers no explanation of it: "The miracle of the appropriateness of the language of mathematics for the formulation of the laws of physics is a wonderful gift which we neither understand nor deserve."

Wigner cites the pragmatist philosopher Charles Sanders Peirce on this:

"The great utility and indispensableness of the conceptions of time, space, and force, even to the lowest intelligence, are such as to suggest that they are the results of natural selection."

...

"Such an hypothesis naturally suggests itself but it must be admitted that it does not seem sufficient to account for the extraordinary accuracy with which these conceptions apply to the phenomena of Nature, and it is probable that there is some secret here which remains to be discovered." [Peirce, 1878].

Another commentator is the mathematician Richard Hamming (1980):

"I have tried, with little success, to get some of my friends to understand my amazement that the abstraction of integers for counting is both possible and useful. Is it not remarkable that 6 sheep plus 7 sheep make 13 sheep; that 6 stones plus 7 stones make 13 stones? Is it not a miracle that the universe is so constructed that such a simple abstraction as a number is possible? To me this is one of the strongest examples of the unreasonable effectiveness of mathematics. Indeed, I find it both strange and unexplainable."

Hamming suggests that the apparent miracle owes something to selection: we pay more attention to situations that are well described by mathematics than to those that are not, and most things are not. But he concludes that the fit, where it happens, still needs an explanation that he can't provide.

A related question is, why are we so completely confident of the predictions that we make by mathematical means? In Hamming's example, why are we so certain that combining a flock of six sheep and a flock of seven sheep will always give a flock of 13 sheep? If we were to try the experiment, and get a different result, we would be sure that we had made a mistake somewhere. Why?

The pioneering developmental psychologist Jean Piaget argued that certain mathematical structures become fundamental to people's reasoning as they mature, changing status from possibilities to inevitable certainties (Piaget, 1971; Piaget and Voyat, 1979). But later work has shown that these certainties can be undermined by contrary evidence. For example, Hall and Kingsley (1968) used covert removal of clay to "show" that rolling a ball of clay into a thin plate made it weigh less, violating the principle of conservation of substance, one of Piaget's structures. Many college students accepted the faked results. Later studies suggest that the details of the inquiries matter, but all show some tendency for adults to accept anomalous results (see, e.g., Winer et al., 1992). So it does not appear that certainty in these matters is securely established during development.

We don't get very much actual data, in the course of everyday life, about the effectiveness of measurement, yet we accept sweeping generalizations about it. For example, we've likely never measured two lengths, one of more than a mile, and one less than a foot, and verified that we can predict their combined length by addition. Yet we believe that we can predict. Why?

The success of measurement consists of a correspondence between entities, relations, and operations in the target domain (the domain of logs, chasms, spanning, and log connectors, for example), and entities, relations, and operations in the representation domain (numbers, greater than, addition). That correspondence is the "structure-preserving mapping" that's the heart of RTM. If the structures in the two domains don't correspond in the right way, the answers we get from measurement won't work in the world.

RTM shows that different measurement systems are possible, as long as these correspondences hold up. For example, it would be possible to measure length in such a way that to predict the length of combined logs, one would *multiply* the lengths of the constituent logs, instead of adding them.

How could this work? One needs a special ruler, marked like the one shown in Figure 1.3, at the top. Note the odd feature that the length of no log at all is not 0, but 1. This is required, because combining no log at all with another log does not change its length, and 1 is the measurement that does that in a multiplicative system, while 0 is the measurement that does that in the familiar way of doing measurement using addition. The lower part of the figure shows a worked example: one log measures 4, with the odd ruler; the second measures 8, and (as predicted) the combined log measures 32.

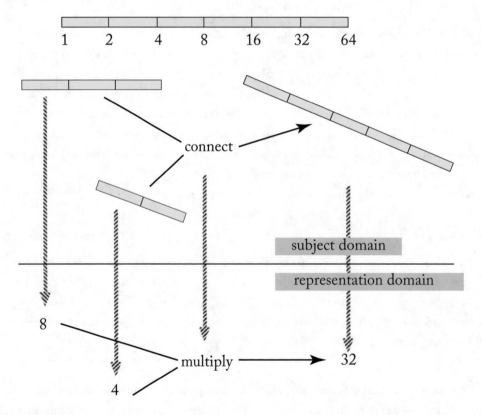

Figure 1.3: Multiplicative measurement of length.

Could one have a system of measurement in which one *subtracts* the lengths of logs to predict their combined lengths? RTM tells us *no*, however strange a ruler we use. The problem is that combining logs is *commutative* where length is concerned: we get the same length if we connect log 1 to log 2, or log 2 to log 1. But the results of subtraction will be different in these cases, so the necessary correspondence does not hold.

RTM deals with numbers and even simpler mathematical systems, like things that can be placed in order, but not used in arithmetic, for example responses chosen from the scale "strongly agree, agree, disagree, strongly disagree." A more general theory of representation needs to relax this restriction, so that we can consider a much wider range of representations. Graphs, sounds, and animations are all possible representations, but aren't simple mathematical objects. We need to allow representation domains that have all these more complex things in them.

Stephen Palmer (1978), in his seminal essay, "Fundamental aspects of cognitive representation", took this step. He analyzed representational systems as containing two worlds, a represented world and a representing world, corresponding to our target and representation domains. And he discussed representing worlds that included such structures as bar charts, or node and link diagrams, and he noted how these systems relate to RTM. Mackinlay and Genesereth (1985) also explored more complex representational systems, followed up by Mackinlay in his dissertation (published as Mackinlay, 1986). While they did not connect their work with RTM, they did develop the principle of corresponding structures, in a different form. They consider *facts* (in a target domain) and statements in a *language* (representation domain). They note that particular structures of facts may not be expressible by statements in a given language, or that expressing some true statements in a language may necessarily also express false ones. These difficulties reflect differences between the structure of the facts and the structure of the language. As in RTM, these structures must match up for the representation scheme to work.

Here's an example of a failure that they use to clarify this point. Suppose one wants to represent relationships among regions in a map, in particular, when one region touches another. One could try to represent each region by a circle, and construct a sentence describing some situation, using the circles, by putting some circles inside others. One could say that region A touches region B, if and only if the circle representing region B is drawn inside the circle for region A, as shown in Figure 1.4.

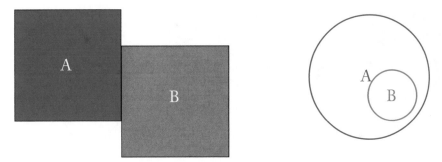

Figure 1.4: Trying to represent touching by nesting.

But this language can't express the facts. In the target domain, if region A touches region B, then region B must touch region A. But in the sentence, only one of these facts can be shown.

In the circle language one has to choose between saying A touches B and B touches A; one can't say both. That's because if A is nested within B, B can't be nested within A, and vice versa. Mathematically, the problem is that touching is a *symmetric* relation A touches B implies B touches A, while nesting is an *antisymmetric* one (A nested in B implies B *not* nested within A).

Box 1.3

One can have fun with Mackinlay and Genesereth's example by changing the use of the circles so as to fix this symmetry problem. Suppose one expresses "A touches B" by requiring *either* that the circle for A is nested in the circle for B, *or* that the circle for B is nested in the circle for A. This revised nesting relation is symmetric, as required.

But Mackinlay and Genesereth point out a further structural problem with the circle language: nesting is *transitive*, while touching is not. That is, if A is nested within B, and B is nested within C, then it follows that A is nested within C. But if region A touches region B, and region B touches region C, it's *not* necessarily the case that region A touches region C.

Does the modified definition of nesting deal with this problem? In part, because the modified relation isn't in general transitive. We could put the circles for A and C next to one another inside the circle for B, as shown in Figure 1.5. Now we have represented the facts that A touches B, and B touches C, but have *not* said that A touches C, because neither is nested within the other.

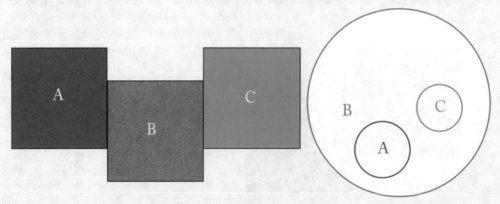

Figure 1.5: Using symmetric nesting to represent touching.

Going further in exploring the modified nesting relation requires that we allow shapes other than circles, so that we can be more flexible in what is nested in what. Doing this allows us to represent the touching in some complex maps, like that of the New England states plus New York, as shown in Figure 1.6.

You can check that all and only the facts about touching are expressed in the diagram using nesting. For example, Maine only touches New Hampshire, because the circle for Maine is only nested within the circle for New Hampshire, and nothing is nested within the circle for Maine.

Does this mean that modified nesting is in fact an adequate representation for touching? No. There are maps it cannot represent. You may want to explore this yourself. Spoiler: the simplest structure that can't be represented with nesting is shown in Figure 1.7.

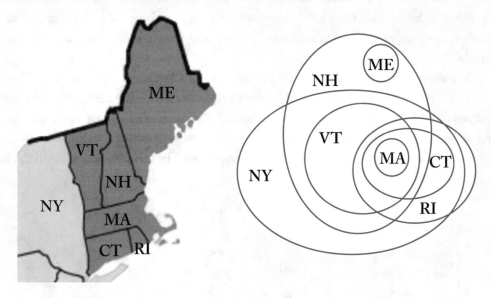

Figure 1.6: Map of New England, and representation of touching using symmetric nesting.

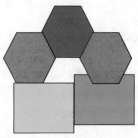

Figure 1.7: A map whose touching cannot be represented with symmetric nesting.

Mackinlay and Genesereth's languages include a wide variety of graphical presentations, more useful than nesting. The point of their analysis isn't to show when representations don't work, but to demonstrate when they do work. They show that a wide range of familiar graphs, like bar graphs and scatter plots, do work to represent a variety of structured data. Such representations can express all the facts of a situation, without implying any false assertions, as required by the principle of structural correspondence.

Mackinlay and Genesereth have taken us far beyond the province of measurement, by considering much more complex representation domains. Mackinlay (1986) makes a further point of fundamental importance: structural correspondence is necessary, but not sufficient, for a representation system to be useful. The added requirement is that it must be possible for someone using a representation to carry out any needed operations, and make any required judgements, easily and accurately.

How might this fail? Mackinlay refers to the work of Cleveland and others (e.g., Cleveland and McGill, 1984) showing that different kinds of graphs place differing demands on the perceptual capabilities of the person viewing them. Figure 1.8 illustrates this point. It shows three bar graphs, drawn differently. All accurately express which of two quantities is larger, because in each case the yellow bar is longer than the red one; bar graphs work by mapping quantities in the target domain to lengths of bars.

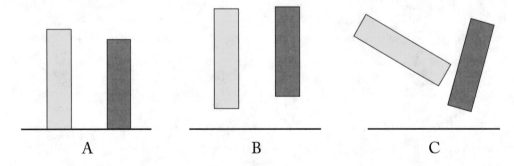

Figure 1.8: Bars that are easily or difficult to compare.

But one can see that these example graphs differ in how easily and accurately the required comparison can be made. When the bases of two bars are aligned, and the bars are parallel, as at A in the figure, the judgment is easy. When the bases are not aligned, and the bars aren't parallel, as at C, the judgement is hard.

Mackinlay calls this further requirement *effectiveness*, adding it to *expressiveness*, the requirement for structural correspondence identified in RTM.

The systems covered by Mackinlay and Genesereth go well beyond the theory of measurement, as we've seen, but there is still more territory to be explored. The languages Mackinlay and Genesereth consider all are static, and all visual. What about animations, and sounds? What does interactivity add? We can frame a still more general theory of representation just by expanding the scope of allowed representational domains to include dynamic structures, interactive systems, and more. This isn't a new theory, but rather the same theory applied to more situations, much as Mackinlay and Genesereth (implicitly) applied RTM to a wider scope, including graphical depictions.

We can further extend the scope of the theory by broadening the idea of the user, in Mackinlay's effectiveness condition. One effect of this is to open the way to consideration of inclusive design, that is, design to support users with a wide range of capabilities. While Mackinlay considers human perceptual capabilities in general, in assessing effectiveness, the logic of his analysis extends equally to the capabilities of particular groups or individuals, which can and do differ. An effective representation must be effective for a particular interpreter, and hence may differ from an effective representation for someone else.

Similarly, without fundamental change to the theory, we can consider other processes than perceptual ones operating on representations. These include cognitive processes: can the user understand the relationships depicted?

It also makes sense to consider computational processes operating on representations, not just operations carried out directly by people. While this needs a more extended treatment than is appropriate here, I've suggested elsewhere (http://comprep.blogspot.com) that computational systems generally provide value because they are representational systems, transforming difficult problems in a very wide range of target domains into tractable problems in computational representational domains. The value of such representations is essentially independent of human perceptual or cognitive capabilities, in general.

I included interactive systems in the list of potential representation domains above. Do these introduce new considerations? To some extent. I'll develop this question when considering our first example, in the next chapter. To foreshadow that discussion, interactive systems include cues for actions in the representation domain, and these cues must be readily interpretable, which does extend the idea of effectiveness somewhat beyond Mackinlay's idea.

1.1   FROM THEORY TO PRACTICE: CREATING A NEW REPRESENTATIONAL SYSTEM, AND USING IT

With this theoretical background in mind, we can outline what is involved in creating a new representational system. We need to have a target domain in mind, since our representational system, to be useful, has to establish a structure preserving mapping between that and some representation domain. But how can we know a target domain, and its structure, without having some kind of representation of it already?

Often, we do use some prior representation in order to know what the structure is. In creating a new representation we are hoping to provide a new representation domain, and a correspondence between that and the target domain, that is easier to work with in some way than what we start with. For example, in representing a collection of numbers as a bar chart, we hope to make it easier to make comparisons. We can do comparisons using the numbers, but using the bars makes it easier. And the numbers tell us enough about the structure of the target domain to allow us to consider alternatives. In working in this way, we are using the layering pattern of representational systems, mentioned earlier, where the representation domain for one system becomes the target domain for another.

Does this mean that there is an infinite regress hiding in the origin of representations? How could there be a *first* representation of something? In some situations the target domain itself can serve as a first representation. In the example of the logs and the chasm, people could accumulate enough experience working directly with logs and combinations of them to discern the structure of the domain. For example, people could see that combining logs is commutative, where what we care about is what gaps the combinations can span.

Another way to get started is by trying out a representation. We may not know up front whether or not a proposed representation actually does capture the structure of the target domain, but experience with it may tell the tale. Some of the examples to come in later chapters have this character. For higher-dimensional structures in space, or musical forms, for example, how well or poorly a proposed representation works may suggest things about the target domain that weren't clear before.

With the target domain in mind, we seek to construct a representation domain, and operations within it, whose structure corresponds to the structure of the target domain, or to what we think we know about the structure. We also have to consider effectiveness: will performing the needed interpretive operations in the representation domain be easy?

Often layering works here, too: if we can map the structure of a target domain onto numbers, we already know lots of ways to represent structures of collections of numbers. And we know that many of these familiar schemes, like bar charts, have reasonable effectiveness.

But, in general, there's no magic here. Indeed, that's why this book is about explorations: there are lots of new domains out there, with new structures, and some may provide useful representations for important target domains.

Once we've created a new representation, how is someone going to learn how to use it? As we've discussed, and as Figure 1.1 shows, representations aren't self-explanatory, considered in isolation.

There's a substantial literature on how people learn to use representations, in the context of math and science learning. Researchers have drawn on a theoretical framework broadly similar to ours, with linked domains. For example, "the most important modeling processes are translations or mappings between contexts" (Lesh, 1981; Goldin and Kaput, 1996) draw specifically on Palmer's two worlds conception (1978).

The picture that emerges is of a *social* process: "the meaning of diagrams, tables, and other displays is established through socially situated efforts to reason with and to interact through artifacts rather than through apprehending self-evident semantic properties of those artifacts (White and Pea, 2011)." That is, people learn to use a new representation by working with it, often along with other people, not from just thinking about the logic of the representation.

The math and science learning literature also includes interesting examples of learners creating new representations. In diSessa et al. (1991), students developed a wide variety of representations of the speed and position of moving objects, using such structures as slanting lines, whose slope represented speed, placed along a horizontal time line. Because these students, sixth graders, did not begin work with a settled understanding of the relationships among time, position, and velocity, their work is an illustration of how trying out representations can be a way to develop one's understanding of the structure of a target domain. Interestingly, working with various representations over a period of days, the students arrived at a graph of position versus time. This arose not as a standard representation provided for them, but as something they evolved from the slanted lines representation, in a social discussion process. Also, interestingly, the students were aware that their representations would not be understood by someone from outside their discussion.

1.2   REPRESENTATIONS AND INCLUSIVE DESIGN

As already discussed, Mackinlay's effectiveness notion can be extended to support people with different capabilities. Whatever operations are required in the representation domain, to accomplish a user's tasks in the target domain, these need to be such that the user can accomplish them easily and accurately. Since people differ in what they can do easily and accurately, it's clear that different representations are required for different people.

Many of the explorations in this book are motivated by this fact. In particular, many of them address the needs of people who can't see well. In many situations the representations in familiar use are visual in character, that is, they require people to perform visual tasks easily and quickly. Plainly such representations aren't useful for people who can't see. The challenge then arises, how can the structure of various target domains, that are usually mapped to visual representation domains, be mapped to representation domains suitable for people who can't see?

Most of the examples in the book use auditory representation domains. There are others, well worth exploring, such as haptic domains that rely on operations of touching or feeling. These aren't explored here, not because they aren't valuable or interesting, but because of a more or less arbitrary choice I've made to focus on representations that can be supported on nearly every machine using a commodity Web browser. There is much more territory than I can explore anyway, so some limitations are unavoidable, and that's one I've chosen.

Of course I can't cover everything within this platform constraint. A very important matter, addressed only very lightly, is that of differences in the cognitive operations required in different representation domains. As already mentioned, in general representations require not only perceptual operations, like comparing the lengths of two bars in a bar graph, but also cognitive operations. I return to this matter briefly in Chapter 2, in considering what has to be understood in using an interactive program.

CHAPTER   2

Interactive Simulation I: Dynamic Electric Field

Let's put the theory of representation to work on an example. We'll start with an existing representation of a complex target domain, the structure of the electric field produced by a moving charge. The representation uses a visual depiction created by Michael Faraday in the early 19th century, *lines of force*. Our aim is to create a *non-visual* representation, one that could be used by a blind learner.

In doing this we'll encounter a variety of issues that have not yet surfaced in our theoretical discussion, including in particular how to describe interactive systems. Because we are constructing a non-visual representation, we'll draw on some guidance for designing *non-visual interactions*.

Radiating Charge (RC; see screenshot in Figure 2.1) is an interactive simulation created by the PhET project at the University of Colorado (https://phet.colorado.edu). You can try the simulation at https://phet.colorado.edu/en/simulation/legacy/radiating-charge. PhET has created some 170 widely used simulations, downloaded at the rate of 75 million times a year. The simulations cover many topics in physics, as well as some in chemistry, biology, and math. Unfortunately, none can be used by blind users. We, and other workers, want to remedy that situation.

As mentioned, RC uses the Faraday lines of force representation of the changing electric field produced by a moving charge. Lines of Force uses the orientation of lines to represent the orientation of the field, and the density of these lines to represent the strength or amplitude of the field. These judgements can't be made by a learner who can't see well.

We could address this difficulty by changing from a visual representation domain, requiring visual judgements, to an auditory domain, requiring auditory judgements. How might this be done?

Here is one way to convey information about the field in an auditory representation. Attending to a particular point in the plane is done visually by directing one's gaze; in the auditory representation (see the program ElectricField, accessed from http://claytonhalllewis.github.io/bookPage.html) one positions an invisible probe to the desired location, using arrow keys. The program announces the x and y coordinates of the probe when it is moved. The orientation of the field at the location of the probe is conveyed by the pitch of a tone. The amplitude is conveyed by the loudness of the tone.

Arguably, this way of representing the field is actually superior to the lines of force method. When one looks at a location on the screen, to determine the orientation of the field at that location from the lines of force, in general no line of force passes through that location. Watching over time, as the lines move, one can notice that a line comes through pointing in some direction, say northeast, and then a little later, one comes through pointing (say) southeast. The next line to arrive points northeast again, and so on. Assuming the situation is continuous, one can imagine that the orientation of the field must be oscillating between those two directions. But this requires reasoning, not simply looking at the lines.

Figure 2.1: Electric field produced by an accelerating charge.

By contrast, in the auditory representation, an oscillating field produces a warbling tone, as the pitch moves up and down, reflecting the shifting orientation. This warbling tone seems to convey oscillation more directly.

The coding of field amplitude as line density is also problematic in the visual form of this simulation. The wavy lines move closer together, or farther apart, as the waves move along, and this makes it hard to tell what the density of the lines is in any region of the display. Here again the auditory presentation, using loudness, can be interpreted more directly.

The program ElectricField actually offers two variants of this representational scheme. In one scheme, called "compass coding" in the program, orientation is mapped to the pitch of the sound in a simple way: the tone when the field points east has a low pitch, which increases smoothly as the orientation shifts around counterclockwise toward north, west, and south. As the orientation nears east, moving up from south, the pitch continues to rise, until it jumps abruptly down to the low tone that represents east. If the orientation shifts from east toward south, the tone similarly abruptly jumps to a high pitch.

These abrupt jumps in pitch can be confusing, when the orientation of the field at the cursor position is oscillating near east. The jumps can be avoided by using a more complex coding scheme that uses Shepard tones (Shepard, 1964), a family of complex sounds that can give the illusion of constantly rising, or constantly falling, indefinitely. The illusion arises from combining several tones with different pitches to form a chord. To produce a rising trend, all the tones are increased in frequency, except that when the topmost tone reaches a maximum it is removed from the chord, and replaced by a tone at the low end of the range used in the coding. To mask the disappearance of a high tone, and its replacement by a low one, the highest and lowest tones are faded in and out. That is, as tones approach the top of the frequency range they are played more and more softly, and when tones are added at the bottom they are initially played very softly, with loudness increasing as their pitch increases.

Using this scheme, the orientation of the field at the location of the cursor is played as one of these chords. If the orientation rotates counterclockwise (an increasing angle), the chords change so as to give the impression of rising; rotation in the other direction gives a falling impression. This can be done so as to convey the fact that the field is oscillating, and whether it is rotating in one direction or the other, with no abrupt jumping anywhere.

This representation of orientation and amplitude does a good job of informing the user of the behavior of the field at any point—perhaps better than the visual presentation, as we've discussed. But it does not convey all the information that a sighted user can obtain from the visual display. What's missing is an impression of the *overall pattern* of disturbances in the field as the charge that produces the field moves. There is no way to coordinate the information obtained when a probe is in one position with that obtained at some other position, because the observations made in different parts of the field will always be obtained at different times.

The visual system performs this comparison automatically, for many positions simultaneously. For example, when viewing the field produced by a charge moving in a circle, one sees a pattern of expanding rings of disturbance, moving out from the center, somewhat like the ripples from a pebble dropped in a pool. A closer look shows that the disturbance is actually a spiral, rather than a pattern of rings.

How could this holistic shape information be conveyed in an auditory representation? One approach, used in ElectricField, is to provide two probes, each of which produces a tone that conveys the orientation and strength of the field at its location. The pitch ranges for the two probes are separated, so that they can be distinguished. Separation of pitch ranges is a powerful cue for sounds being attributed to distinct sources, called *auditory stream segregation*, as articulated in research on *auditory scene analysis.* Albert Bregman, the founder of this area of research, has wonderful demonstrations online at http://webpages.mcgill.ca/staff/Group2/abregm1/web/index.htm.

Using this representation it is possible to distinguish a pattern of rings from a spiral, by placing the two probes on opposite sides of the "screen," equidistant from the origin. One can hear that the pitch changes at these two locations are out of phase (that is, one probe is giving a rising tone when the other is falling). But concentric rings would produce changes that are in phase, for points equidistant from the origin, moving up and down at exactly the same time.

While this discrimination using two probes is possible, it is far from obvious. Like the interpretation of the lines of force representation, it requires reasoning rather than simple perception.

How could the pattern of the disturbance be conveyed more directly, in auditory form? We'll return to this question in Chapter 8, where we consider how dynamic spatial information might be conveyed with music.

2.1   INTERACTING WITH THE SIMULATION

The simulation ElectricField provides a menu system to allow the user to interact with the simulation via a number of actions. It thus provides a good example with which to consider the representational issues that are involved in representations that are *interactive*, rather than simply being presented to a user.

We can note that the actions supported in this simulation are of different kinds, viewed within the context of the representational system. Some actions in the simulation correspond to actions in the *target domain*: for example, one can change the way the charge is moving, from stationary, to circular, vertical, or horizontal. Other actions have no effect in the target domain, but modify the *representation domain*. For example, one can choose between compass coding and Shepard coding. This changes nothing in the target domain, but does change the representation domain from one in which field orientation is mapped to the frequency of a simple tone, to one in which it is mapped to a Shepard tone.

Other actions change nothing in either the target domain or the representation domain, but simply *provide information*. For example, there is a command that causes the simulation to announce the coordinates of the probes in the target domain.

Let's call all these actions, those that act on, or provide information about, the target or representation domains, *primary* actions. We'll see that there is another representation domain that represents these primary actions, and that there are further actions, let's call them *secondary* actions, that act on this further representation domain.

So we have actions that relate in various different ways to the target and representation domain of the simulation. To make sense of this diversity we need to consider some complications in the structure of representational systems that we haven't needed until now.

One common complication is *combination*, in which a representational system is formed by combining two simpler ones. That's at work here: there's a representational system that uses simple compass coding for orientation, and there's one that uses Shepard coding. We could certainly have one or the other of these, on its own. But the simulation we are examining includes *both*, as sketched in Figure 2.2. There we can see that the needed structural correspondence between target and representation domains consists of two sets of mappings, one for the compass representation and one for the Shepard representation.

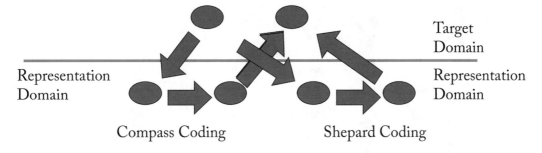

Figure 2.2: A target domain mapped to two representation domains.

Another common complication, that we've seen before, is layering. Many representational systems have several domains layered on top of one another, as shown in Figure 2.3. Here there is one target domain at the top, the one we ultimately care about. It's been mapped to a representation domain, just beneath. But then that domain is treated as the target domain for another layer of representation, and mapped to a second representation domain. That one serves as the target for a yet lower representation, and so on.

To the right in Figure 2.3 the layers in some common stacks of representations are named. For example, many physical problems are represented by equations in physics, then these are mapped to mathematical expressions, and these expressions are mapped to programs in some programming language. Then these programs are mapped to instructions for some computer, and these instructions are mapped to the states of electronic circuits in a computer. The mappings at all levels are contrived so that the action of the circuits in the program produce results that correspond to desired answers to questions in the top level target domain, the physical system.

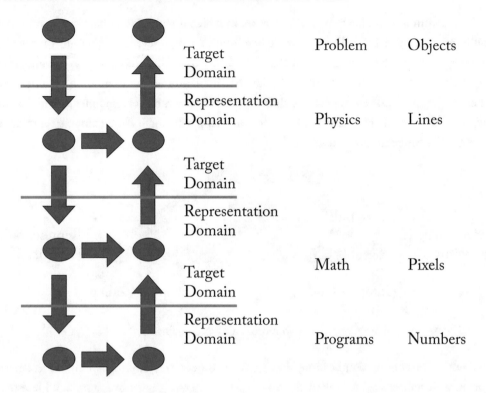

Figure 2.3: How representations are layered, with some examples.

Another common layer structure has as its target domain objects in space, with these mapped to geometric forms like lines, which are then mapped to patterns of color and brightness in a grid of picture elements, which are in turn mapped to triples of numbers. This stack can be extended downward: the numbers are represented by, bits in a binary representation of the numbers, and then to the states of electronic circuits representing those bits. This stack of layers is useful because there are operations on the circuits, carried easily by programs, that can produce effects that correspond to desired operations on the original objects in space.

More detailed analysis of either of these examples would reveal cases of combination, as well as layering. For example, computer systems have more than one way of mapping numbers to bits, one that's adapted to exact representation of whole numbers, and one that's adapted to good approximations to continuous quantities, over a wide range of sizes. Both are commonly used within the same program.

We need these complications to analyze the actions in the electric field simulation that do not connect to the target or representation domain, the secondary actions. Figure 2.4 sketches the situation, in two steps. Figure 2.4a shows the main outline of the combined representational system that offers a choice or compass or Shepard coding. It also shows two actions, changing the motion of the charge (acting in the representation domain), and selecting which coding to use, acting in the representation domain.

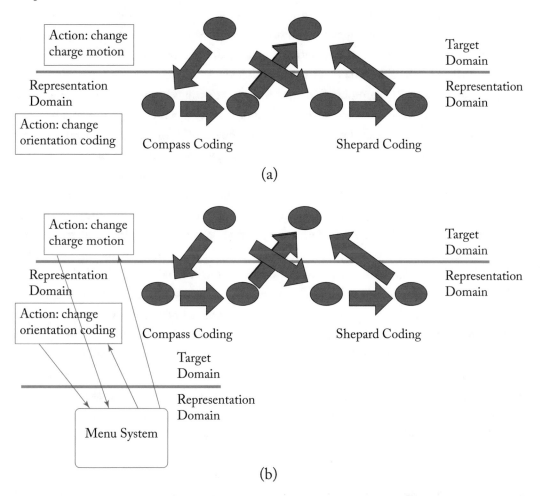

Figure 2.4: (a) Two actions in the simulation and (b) representing actions using a menu system.

Figure 2.4b completes the picture. It adds another layer to the representational system, in which the actions in the representation domain form the target domain, and a new representation is provided for them: a *menu system*.

What's the point of that? As for any representational system, the idea is that working in the representation domain, with the menu, will be easier than working directly with the actions in the target domain, which in this case is sometimes the target domain of the overall system, and sometimes in its representation domain. The menu maps the target actions onto convenient keyboard actions that select them. And, importantly, it provides *descriptions* of the actions, and a way to move around among the available actions, so that we can more easily find and select the actions we want.

The value of looking at the representational system in this more complex way is that it allows us to work on the key issues in any representational system, expressiveness, that is, structural correspondence between target and representation domains, and effectiveness, that is, whether desired results can easily be obtained in the representation domain.

Expressiveness isn't a big problem in representing the actions in the example simulation. The actions are discrete, and can easily be mapped to simple choices in a menu. But it would be a problem, if one wanted to capture all the features of the original PhET simulation, which the example simulation doesn't try to do. For example, the original simulation doesn't just allow the learner to choose among a list of alternative motions for the charge, it allows the learner to generate an arbitrary motion. The original does this using a mouse action that can't easily be supported without visual guidance, and the example simulation is designed not to need that. That is, the *potential* target domain for the example simulation includes actions that are *not* expressed by the representation domain used for actions in the example simulation. That is, the representation domain used in ElectricField cannot *express* all the actions that are possible in the original PhET simulation.

Effectiveness raises a longer list of key questions, of three kinds. First, do the descriptions provided for actions work as they need to? That is, can learners understand what the choices will do, and, if they want to do something, can they identify the correct choice to do that? Second, can users easily navigate among the choices? The descriptions will affect this, of course, but even if the descriptions are good it could be hard or easy to move among the choices. Finally, how are the answers to these first two questions affected by the capabilities of the user? In particular, for our example, it's crucial that people who can't see be able to understand the actions, from the spoken descriptions, and that they be able to navigate easily, with just the spoken output the menu system provides.

We can see that these considerations are not only perceptual in character, but also cognitive. There is a lot to understand, not just the meaning of the descriptions that are provided, but also the meaning of the actions in the target domain that are represented by the choices in the menu system. Just as some people have difficulty in perceiving information presented in particular ways, some people will have difficulty with the cognitive demands of a particular system, both because of the demands of the interface (understanding the descriptions, in this case) and in terms of understanding the target domain. Understanding these cognitive aspects of effectiveness is important new ground for the design of representations. Explorations are needed!

Box 2.1

Effectiveness from a Broader Perspective: Cognitive Dimensions Analysis

Adding "understanding" to the list of things one may need to do with a representation only scratches the surface. The variety is enormous. One may be simply trying to understand something, or answer some question about it, but one may also be trying to modify a structure, or create a new one. Or one may need to compare two structures. The character of these activities will be affected not only by the nature of the representation domain, but also by the nature of the target domain. Different representations impose, or avoid, a wide range of difficulties in this landscape of tasks.

Thomas Green and his students and collaborators have created a remarkable catalog of these difficulties, called Cognitive Dimensions of Notations. The catalog lists 14 categories of things that can work well or badly in working with representational systems of many kinds.

For example, viscosity is resistance to change. In some representations it is easy to modify a structure, while in others it is difficult. One common source of viscosity is *hidden dependencies*. It may be that if I want to change some feature X, I also need to change Y, because X depends on Y in some way. But if the dependency is hidden, I won't see that I need to change Y.

The catalog, with extensive supporting resources, is available online at http://www. cl.cam.ac.uk/~afb21/CognitiveDimensions/, maintained by Alan Blackwell, one of Green's students, and himself a leading exponent of the Cognitive Dimensions work. A valuable feature of the catalog is that it includes suggested workarounds and remedies for the difficulties, so that one can not only understand one's problems better but also fix them.

The menu system in the example is strongly shaped by design guidance provided by Sina Bahram, an experienced designer of inclusive systems. Sina's guidance is published as Section 2.2 of Wyman et al. (2016); here are some of the key points.

Descriptions should be ordered so that more specific information precedes more general. Auditory presentations are slow, because one can't skim over them as rapidly as is possible with visual skimming of a text or a visible layout of controls. It's important to give the user the information they need to make a choice as quickly as possible. Presenting specific information first allows them to move along, without waiting for the generalities, or to stay longer, if they wish, to get more complete information.

The reading of descriptions as synthetic speech must be nonblocking. That is, if the user navigates to the next item, the description of the next item should start without waiting for the previous description to be read.

Lists of choices should wrap around at the ends, using a nonspeech sound to indicate when that happens. If navigation is blocked at the end of list, users have to waste time running into the block. Further, wraparound makes it faster to move from one end of a list to the other. Nonspeech sounds can be identified more quickly than speech sounds, so they make it easier and faster to tell that one has wrapped around.

The keyboard navigation commands in the menus make heavy use of the arrow keys. Broadly, the keys are used as if the choices in a top level menu are arranged horizontally, as if they formed a menu bar, so that the left and right arrows are used to move among these choices. Submenus are accessed using the up and down keys, as if they were arranged vertically. Each menu item is read when the user navigates to it.

Some of the actions set values for attributes of the simulation, like the orientation coding. The current value of these attributes is read when the user navigates to the corresponding item in the menu bar, so they know the current value.

This use of arrow keys is intended to assist the user in conceiving the program and associated structures in a spatial arrangement, even though the arrangement is wholly invisible. This idea is borrowed from a popular Twitter client for blind users, TWBlue, as suggested by Sina.

The scheme can be described as *pseudospatial navigation*, rather than simply spatial, because the implicit geometry suggested by the directional movements departs from that in a real space. Wraparound is one example of a violation of true spatiality: by moving "down" repeatedly, past the end of a menu, one finds oneself at the "top." Similarly, moving repeatedly to the "right" can take one back to the "left" end of the menu bar.

How clear, or how confusing, this scheme is must be determined by user experience. But there is reason to believe that users will tolerate the spatial distortions that the scheme entails. Research by Zetzsche and collaborators (Zetzsche et al., 2007) shows that sighted users, navigating a virtual environment on a computer screen, are equally well able to learn to move in geometrically impossible environments as in possible ones. An example of such an impossible environment is shown in Figure 2.5. In that environment, if you move some distance south, then turn east, and then go a short distance directly north, you get back to the top, even though in reality, if you moved in that way, you'd have to end up some way southeast of your start. Zetzsche et al. also found that even topologically impossible environments are readily learned, for example one in which there are paths that run from the inside to the outside of a closed contour, without crossing the contour, and without passing above or below. Further, participants not only could learn to navigate these impossible spaces, but also could not reliably discriminate impossible spaces from possible ones, when asked to do so. These findings suggest not only that people may be able to work effectively in a distorted, pseudospatial navigation scheme, but also that they may not notice anything anomalous about it.

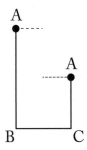

Figure 2.5: An impossible environment: the locations marked A are the same, although the path shown could not possibly return to its start. Based on Zetzsche et al., 2007, Figure 2.

This question of spatial understanding, or confusion, falls within Mackinlay's consideration of effectiveness, as suggested earlier in this discussion. We have a representation of the primary actions in ElectricField that adequately expresses the structure of those actions. But its effectiveness, or lack of effectiveness, will be determined by the spatial reasoning capabilities of users, not by its abstract structure.

2.2   MODEL AND VIEWS

Many computer scientist readers will be familiar with design patterns that couple a model with one or more *views*, a way to separate content from presentation, as mentioned in the Preface. This first example illustrates this pattern in its handling of orientation coding: users can select one of two views of the same model, one using compass coding and one using Shepard coding. The simulation code is structured in such a way that the same model is used in both cases: there's just an angle computed at each point at each instant. The two views present this angle to the user in different ways. The value of the separation between model and view is that other views could easily be added, with no need to modify the code for the model at all.

This separation, while usually desirable in any situation, is especially important for inclusive design. People have diverse perceptual abilities, and so (as we've seen) representations that are effective for one person maybe ineffective for others. The easier it is to add additional views, the easier it will be to support a wide range of users.

Substituting views is easy in simple cases like the one here. More generally, adding a new presentation, that perhaps requires different information from a model, is a significant challenge, and may require a lot of code to be modified. Because of this, only the original creator of a program may be able to add views, whereas ideally it should be possible for anyone to add a new view if they need one. The Fluid Infusion project is doing pathbreaking work in developing new software structures that make this kind of flexibility possible; see Basman et al., (2016) and Clark and Basman (2017).

CHAPTER 3

Interactive Simulation II: Balloons and Static Electricity

Balloons and Static Electricity (https://phet.colorado.edu/en/simulation/balloons-and-static-electricity; see Figure 3.1) is another of the PhET sims, with more narrative content than the Radiating Charge example we've been working with. That is, one can tell a causal story about what's happening: you rub a balloon on the sweater; negative charges stick to the balloon; when the balloon is moved away, and released, it's attracted back to the sweater. Other events occur when the balloon in moved near the wall: its charges rearrange the charges in the wall so that it sticks there.

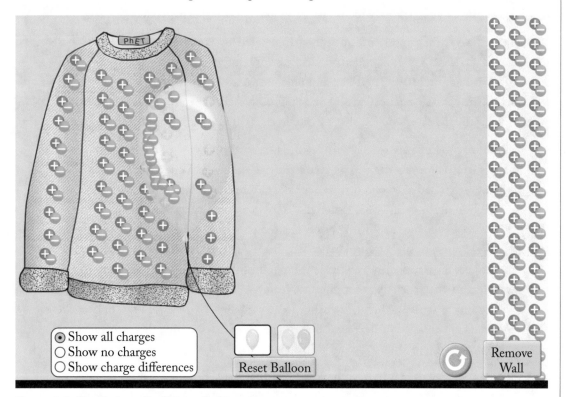

Figure 3.1: Simulation of rubbing a balloon on a sweater.

Work by Smith and collaborators (Moore and Lewis, 2015; Smith et al., 2016a, 2016b, 2017) shows how the interactive visual representation in this simulation can be supplemented by spoken descriptions to allow a blind user to follow what is going in. These spoken descriptions are delivered to a blind learner via their screen reader, a program that uses synthesized speech to "read" information that might be presented visually on the screen.

Box 3.1

Screen Reader Programs

When synthetic speech technology became widely available, in the early 1980's, it became possible for a computer to render textual information in spoken form, rather than showing it visually (by printing, or using a computer display.) Programs to do this came to be called "screen readers," because their effect was more or less to read aloud information that was displayed on the computer screen. In fact, the programs do not read the screen itself; rather, they read information in the screen buffer, a data structure inside the computer from which the display on the screen is generated.

In the days when most information manipulated by computers was textual, these screen reader programs provided good access for blind users. But the emergence of the graphical user interface (GUI), beginning concurrently with the development of early screen reader software, called for new approaches. When information is presented graphically the screen buffer does not contain text that the screen reader can speak.

There are two basic approaches that modern screen readers use to deal with this issue. One is to look for descriptive text accompanying an image. When this is provided, by whomever created the content that includes the image, the screen reader speaks the description. But not all visual material a computer can display is made up of images. Structures like menus and dialog boxes are also presented visually, and some means of rendering these in spoken form is needed. This issue is addressed by asking program- mers to use an accessibility Application Program Interface (API), a collection of soft- ware features for specifying user interface features like menus and dialog boxes. When a programmer creates a menu, say, using an accessibility API, the API not only creates the visual presentation of the menu, but also provides a description that a screen reader program can use to render the menu in spoken form.

Besides collaborators using synthetic speech to provide a non-visual presentation of material that might otherwise be presented visually, screen reader programs also help users navigate within the material, that is, to control what part of it is read out, and when. Because speaking and listening are almost entirely serial processes, that is, one can't speak two things at once, or easily listen to two things at once, it is difficult to get an overview of a page full of information, the way a sighted reader might do in skimming text. Screen readers help with this by providing commands that quickly skip from heading to heading in a page. If the headings are well written, this can greatly speed access to the content, as the user can use the headings to locate the parts that are of interest. Commands are also provided to move quickly among the various controls that a program may present, menus, dialog boxes, and so on, and to operate on them. There are many demonstrations of screen reader use on YouTube that will give you a sense of how these features work.

As you can see in the demos, skilled screen reader users speed up their access to information in another way, by exploiting the ability of synthetic speech technology to speak at very high rates. While a common speech rate for a person speaking conversational English is about 150 words per minute, a screen reader user may set their speech synthesizer's rate at 450 words per minute.

These features of modern screen readers can provide their users with good access to much online content and many tools and services. But, unfortunately, the access depends on the people who create the content and services doing the right things, and too often they don't. For example, if images aren't accompanied by descriptions, or a document doesn't include headings, or a software tool does not use an accessibility API, access will be difficult.

For more about the history of screen reader technology, see Lazzaro (1990) and Schwerdtfeger (1991). For a more complete description of screen reader capabilities, and related considerations for people creating online content and services, see WebAIM (2017).

Because the original simulation doesn't present information textually, descriptions have to be added. Further, to allow the screen reader to locate, and then describe, some pieces of the simulation, a new data structure was added to the program to hold representations of these pieces. This added data structure, called a "parallel document object model" (parallel DOM), is necessary because some things that appear on the screen in the original simulation exist only as images created by the software, that the screen reader can't access.

With this enhancement, the same simulation can be used by sighted and non-sighted learners. This is very desirable in a learning situation in which learners with different capabilities are working together, as they might in a group problem solving or discussion activity in a classroom.

Smith and collaborators found that learners need different kinds of descriptive information, accessed in different ways. One kind is information about the situation being simulated, and the available controls, that doesn't change: there is a balloon, there is a sweater, there is a wall; there is a button to grab the balloon. Other information changes: there are negative charges here, or there. Still other information describes something that happens when the user takes an action: for example, when the balloon is released, it moves to the sweater. The learner wants to know this as it happens.

It makes sense to access these forms of information in different ways. The information that doesn't change (*static* information) forms an outline that the learner can navigate with their screen reader. It's always available for review in a fixed arrangement. Dynamic information, information that changes as the simulation runs, is attached to this outline, so it too can be accessed by navigating to it using the screen reader, and the current state of any part of the simulated situation can be reviewed that way at any time.

Information about the immediate effects of learner actions are presented differently, as *alerts*. That is, when the learner does something that has an immediate effect, a description of the effect is read to them right away. They don't have to navigate anywhere, or make a request, to get this information.

Access for learners who can't see requires other features that simulations for sighted learners often don't include. A sighted learner will move the balloon by dragging it with mouse; a learner who can't see can't do that (and, in general, can't use the mouse at all, because the mouse pointer has to be tracked visually in nearly all uses of a mouse.) This requires the simulation to support *keyboard access*, meaning that all commands can be executed by keyboard operations not requiring the mouse. The descriptions the simulation provides have to include the information about these keyboard operations, as well as about the state of the situation being simulated.

Keyboard access is important for other aspects of inclusion, as well. Some sighted learners have motor limitations that prevent their using the mouse. They may not be able to use the keyboard, either, but special hardware connected to the computer can allow them to control a program in other ways, for example by eye movements, as long as all commands can be issued via the computer's keyboard interface.

3.1   PERSPECTIVE FROM THEORY OF REPRESENTATIONS

Comparing the presentation of the sim for blind learners with that for sighted learners, we see that the use of a screen reader makes a huge difference. The representation domain has shifted to the domain of spoken linguistic expressions from that of moving pictures. There are also differences in how actions are carried out and how they are cued; cuing also has changed to language (hearing a description of a keyboard command) from pictures (seeing a button); we discussed these matters in the previous chapter.

One can ask how well the target domain, the evolution of the situation that includes the balloon, the sweater, and the wall, lends itself to representation in these two domains. As we saw in the previous chapter, it can be argued that the target domain for the electric field simulation considered in the previous chapter does *not* lend itself to linguistic simulation; it exhibits complex patterns of movement that are not easy to describe. On the other hand, the events in Balloons and Static Electricity seem to have a simple narrative character—you rub the balloon on the sweater, charges are picked up, you move the balloon away, you release it, it flies back to the sweater. It's plausible that little of importance is lost in describing these events in words, rather than showing them in pictures.

What about the other sims in the PhET collection? Are these mostly like the electric field simulation, with complex visual patterns, or do they have simple narrative structure? A sample of about a third of the 130 some simulations shows that very few have the kind of narrative structure that Balloons and Static Electricity has. On the other hand, something over half present complex visual patterns.

The majority of the simulations that are complex visually present a particular form of visual pattern: quantitative graphs, that show plots of various quantities as they are affected by the physical situation being depicted, and the learner's interactions with it. The problem of presenting quantitative graphs non-visually is much studied, though no clearly superior technique has emerged. Useful approaches include tactile presentation (see, for example, Giudice et al., 2012), sonification, for example using rising and falling pitches to convey the shape of a curve in a graph (e.g., Walker and Mauney, 2010), and generating linguistic descriptions of a shape of a curve (e.g., Carberry at al., 2004). Continued work on making the whole collection of PhET simulations accessible will need to explore these approaches.

CHAPTER   4

Amodal Representations for Interactive Simulations

The development of a more inclusive version of the simulation in the last chapter follows a pattern that's common in such work. One starts with a representation that's been developed for sighted learners, and then works to provide access to that representation, generally via a screen reader. Distinguished blind computer scientist T.V. Raman called for a different approach: developing representations for blind users that relate directly to the underlying content, not to a representation created for sighted people (Raman, 1996; Raman and Gries, 1997). Jason White of Educational Testing Service (personal communication, Princeton, NJ, December 9, 2014) has suggested that this might be done by creating a fundamentally *amodal* representation of the content, that is, a representation not linked to any particular concrete presentation, or any sensory modality, such as sight or hearing. Different presentations of this amodal representation, for different users or usage situations, for example visual or auditory representations, or ones adapted for use on small screens, could then be created.

This idea conforms to an often-stated principle of computer science, that we've mentioned earlier: separation of content and presentation. In 1984, as the graphical user interface was coming into its own, John Seely Brown criticized then-popular What You See is What You Get (WYSIWYG) editors on the grounds that they entangled the content of a document with its appearance, offering immediate apparent benefits to document creators but actually limiting what could later be done with the content (Brown, 1984).

Brown's concern was borne out by experience with making documents accessible to blind readers. Often a document is prepared in such a way that it *looks* well structured, that is, its structure is adequately signaled to sighted readers, but the structure is not represented in the content, and is thus difficult to recover for non-visual presentations. In particular, as we saw earlier, for good access, headings in a document must be marked in a way that a screen reader can recognize. But a document can *look* as if it has headings that divide it into sections—some text is in a larger font, and bolded—but not use the particular markings that a screen reader looks for. Thus the structure of the document is conveyed only visually.

If Hypertext Markup Language (HTML) is used to create a document, and used properly, the structure of the document is specified in a way that is not tied to visual presentation. HTML includes markings called *tags* that can indicate what pieces of text are headings, and what level of heading they are. This information can be used to generate a visual presentation, with headings shown in a larger font, and bolded, say. But it can also be used by a screen reader to create a spoken presentation that can be navigated in a way the reflects the underlying structure.

In this sense, the HTML representation of the document is *amodal*. Its specification of the structure of the document does not rely on visual cues, nor on spoken ones; rather, its representation can be used to produce other representations in those modalities, or in others. Similarly, HTML allows one to create controls, like buttons or hyperlinks. These, too, can be rendered as visual representations, to be clicked using a mouse, or a touch screen. But they can also be rendered as spoken descriptions, to be operated by keypresses.

Box 4.1

Can representations be truly amodal?

Since any representational system includes a representation domain, might one argue that any representation must be modal, in the sense that it is tied to its representation domain, whatever that is? I have two responses. First, for our purposes we need only a narrow sense of modality, tied to human sensory functions, such as sight or hearing. I think we can agree that if we represent something like an orientation using a number, the representation is amodal in this narrow sense. We can represent the number visually, in many different ways, or auditorily, in many different ways, or by a haptic display, but the number itself has meaning independent of any of these. Similarly, as we've seen, a heading or a button, specified in HTML, has meaning independent of any particular presentation of it, visual or non-visual.

The second response may be more controversial: we may conceive of representations that are not only amodal in the sense of being free of any connection to a sensory modality, but in fact free of a dependence on any particular representation domain at all. Here numbers can also serve as an example. There are indefinitely many ways we can represent a number, but none of these is what the number *is*. Rather, we have an idea of the number that is closer to what all of these representations have in common.

The philosopher Paul Benacerraf (1965) explores this matter in his paper, "What Numbers Could Not Be." He imagines an argument breaking out between two children, each of whom has been taught a different model of the natural numbers, one due to Zermelo, and one due to von Neumann. The argument is about whether or not 3 belongs to 17. This crazy-seeming question arises, because in both models the numbers are identified with certain sets, and in the von Neumann model 3 does belong to 17, and in the other it does not. Benacerraf's point is that neither model tells us what the numbers "really are." But this in no way prevents us from feeling that we know what numbers are, well enough to work with them.

These reflections suggest that our understanding of things is commonly not captured in a single representational system, but many, used in concert. The representation domain in this composite system is complex, and indefinite: we may add a new representational subsystem to it at any time. Many of the subsystems will be modal in the narrow sense of being tied to some sensory modality. Others will be modal in the broader sense of using some specific representational domain. But taken as a whole the composite system is amodal even in the wider sense.

Coming back down to earth, do these considerations apply to HTML? An argument that they don't comes from the technical fact that the tags in HTML must consist of certain specified characters, so that these characters define a "mode" to which HTML is necessarily tied, even if the entities like headings and buttons may be rendered in indefinitely many ways. But taking a wider view, we could imagine severing this tie. In some future technology we may find that we need to replace the familiar bits of today with continuous analog quantities, accompanied by some way to map these quantities to the behavior of programs that render HTML structures for us. In this new technology there might be no things that correspond uniquely to the characters in today's HTML tags. But we might feel that this new system is still "HTML." We'd feel that way because of the overlap between the old system and the new, in the way we reason about them and work with them.

If we accept that we can have amodal representations of things like documents, can we do the same for more complex things, like interactive simulations? What could such an abstract, amodal representation actually be?

For science simulations, a possible answer to this question is provided by the idea of "mechanism," suggested by philosopher and historian of science Lindley Darden and her collaborators (Machamer et al., 2000; Darden, 2002). Mechanisms in Darden's sense are "Entities and activities organized such that they are productive of regular changes from start or set-up to finish or termination conditions" (Machamer et al., 2000, p. 3). Darden finds that scientists seek to describe the evolution of situations by a chain of mechanisms, each creating the conditions that enable the next one to act. Mechanisms can be seen as units of scientific understanding: a phenomenon or process is fully understood when it can be completely described by mechanisms. For example, the supply of oxygen to the cells of the body can be described as the action of a mechanism that draws air into the lungs, a mechanism that binds oxygen to hemoglobin molecules in cells in the blood, a mechanism that pumps the blood out into the body, and a mechanism that transfers oxygen from the hemoglobin to a cell in the body. Often mechanisms can be subdivided into mechanisms at a lower level, supporting explanations with more or less detail, with mechanisms that are more or less complex.

While Darden is describing scientific research, the mechanisms idea can be adapted to describe aspects of science learning. Just as researchers seek to develop a complete understanding of a situation in terms of mechanisms, so science learners seek to develop such an understanding. An interactive simulation can be seen as a means of supporting the identification of mechanisms at work in the situation. It therefore seems promising to consider whether the evolution of a situation in a simulation can be described by specifying the mechanisms needed to account for it. That is, one seeks a collection of mechanisms adequate to determine what should happen in response to any given user actions executed during a simulation session. The best test of this adequacy would be that the mechanisms can actually be executed, so that the simulation can actually be implemented simply as a collection of mechanisms, where these produce all of the phenomena characteristic of the situation being simulated.

While Darden and colleagues have not formalized the idea of mechanism, it is easy to see that it corresponds in a simple way to the condition-action rule formalism common in many computational models of reasoning. Such models consist of a collection of data of some kind, and a collection of rules, each of which has a *condition*, that is, an expression that may be true or false of the data, and an action, that is an expression that specifies some change to the data. At any moment a rule whose condition is true of the data can *apply*, meaning that its action is carried out, producing a change in the data.

Like mechanisms, rules can act in sequence. One rule can modify the data in such a way that another rule can apply. A collection of rules can thus specify how a situation evolves, with the data at each moment reflecting the changing state of the situation. User actions in an interactive situation can be modeled as changes to the data, as well, so that how the situation evolves is determined not just by the rules that represent the mechanisms at work, but also by the effects of user actions.

A system of this kind is amodal, in that the rules and the data they operate on are not linked to a presentation in any particular sensory modality. But presentations can readily be added, in at least two ways.

First, a program can be added that creates a concrete presentation of the state of the data at any moment. If this presentation is visual, say showing pictures of objects involved in the situation, in different locations, the result is close to that given by a conventional visual interactive simulation. One sees objects moving about and changing form. The program Amodal shows such a visual representation for the Balloons and Static Electricity simulation described in Chapter 3. Figure 4.1 shows a screen shot of the program.

Figure 4.1: Visual presentation of an amodal simulation. A balloon, with some charged particles shown, has picked up an electron from a sweater. The structure at right suggests the random arrangement of charged particles in a wall. Buttons at the top of screen are used to trigger actions with a hand, shown holding the balloon.

There are some differences between this visual presentation and the original. One is that user actions are reduced to button presses rather than being executed by dragging. A second, related, difference is that objects move abruptly rather than by smooth animation as in the existing PhET simulation. This also is a consequence of the simple model of spatial position used in the program, in which only discrete locations are represented. A more sophisticated spatial model could address this limitation.

A second way to add a concrete presentation is also demonstrated by Amodal, in the form of synthesized speech, giving a non-visual presentation. Rather than being driven by changes in the data in the model as the simulation runs, this spoken presentation is derived from the actions of the mechanisms themselves, that is, by the rules that represent the mechanisms.

This is accomplished by adding an extra action to each rule that generates a description of what the mechanism does. For example, a rule that transfers an electron from the sweater to the balloon, when the balloon is rubbed on the sweater, generates this description: "If a balloon is rubbed on something with an electron, the electron moves onto the balloon."

The mechanisms version of Balloons and Static electricity requires 16 rules. Of these, six are concerned with opening and closing the hand, and moving objects held in the hand. Thus, just ten rules are needed to capture the physics content. Of these, five clearly describe mechanisms, that is, changes to the situation under specified conditions. In words, these are:

1. transport an electron from sweater to balloon, when rubbing;

2. attracted object moves if light and not held;

3. object drops if not held and not attracted.;

4. object with electron deficit rotates dipoles in wall; and

5. dipoles in wall drift to random position in absence of nearby charge.

The remaining five rules have a different status. They don't describe changes in the situation, but rather changes in how the situation is *described*. For example, one rule acts when the balloon is moved away from a location on the sweater, and adds an indication in the data that the balloon has been rubbed. There is some scientific knowledge embedded here: it could be important to know that it's the breaking of contact between the balloon and the sweater that's important about rubbing. But there is no change of state of the situation.

Another example of this kind of rule is one that determines that an attraction exists between something with an electron deficit and something with an electron surplus. This rule, too, encodes some scientific knowledge, but it does not specify any change in the situation. The attraction already existed as soon as the deficit and surplus were created.

The other "descriptive" rules do the following:

• define when an object has an electron deficit: part of it has a proton and no electron;

• define when an object has an electron surplus: part of it has an electron and no proton; and

• define that an attraction exists between something with an electron surplus and the rotated dipoles nearby.

Since the descriptive rules do not specify changes of state, could they be dispensed with? Yes and no. More complex rules could be written that combine the descriptive rules with the rules for the mechanisms for which the descriptions are currently used. For example, the rule that makes something move when attracted could have in its condition not the presence of an attraction, but rather the conditions under which the presence of an attraction is noticed.

This seems undesirable, however. Not only would the rules become more complex, but also more would be needed. Even in this small simulation there is more than one way an attraction can arise (between surplus and deficit or between surplus and rotated dipoles), but some effects of the attraction are the same in both cases. Linking the effects of an attraction directly to all of the possible means of producing an attraction misses what all these situations have in common.

Taking stock, we now have an example of an amodal representation of the content of a simulation, in terms of mechanisms (and associated descriptive rules). We have two presentations generated from this amodal representation, one visual and one using synthetic speech. What advantages might this approach to inclusion have for such simulations?

First, the work of specifying the content of the simulation is completely shared among any presentations we might create. For example, we might seek to create representation for people with vision limited in some particular way. No work on the content of the simulation, but only on the presentation of it, would be needed.

Second, the amodal representation opens up other kinds of diversity in presentation. In fact, this diversity is suggested by the two example presentations we've discussed. The visual presentation, like the original, shows only the effects of the mechanisms at work. Things just move in response to user actions. The presentation doesn't suggest anything about the mechanisms themselves. The presentation using synthetic speech is quite different. Because the presentation is generated by the rules that specify the mechanisms, it is easy and natural for the presentation to include a full explanation, saying not just what happened, but why (within the limitations of the mechanisms as specified).

Is this desirable? One line of argument suggests that it is. If Darden is right, then one can say that understanding a simulation means understanding the mechanisms involved, and so a presentation that supports identifying these is important. Certainly explicit description of them is one way to provide this support.

On the other hand, just presenting these explanations, wordy as they are, may be pedagogically disastrous. The pedagogy developed by the PhET project is strongly nondirective (Adams et al., 2008), aiming to allow learners to discover things for themselves. Just telling things can suffer from the well-known disadvantages of *instructivism*, including learners staying passive. As Adams et al. say, "Our instincts and training may lead us to 'tell' students about science and math as we understand it. Unfortunately research has shown that simply telling is not always the most effective way to share our understanding."

The amodal presentation opens up interesting possible responses. One is, of course, simply not to describe the mechanisms, but only their effects, reflecting the design of current PhET simulations. This could readily be done in synthetic speech, producing it in the same way as the visual presentation in the example program, by describing the data as the simulation runs. But it would also be possible to place more complete explanations under the control of the learner or of the teacher. Explanations could be provided for some aspects of the simulation and not others, so that learners can focus their attention on exploring just some mechanisms.

Another possibility is providing explanations of the same phenomena at different levels. The rules in this program do not address why it is that something with an electron surplus is attracted to something with an electron deficit and, in fact, says nothing about the facts underlying this phenomenon. The rules are: that electrons repel one another; that protons repel one another to exactly the same extent; and that an electron and a proton attract one another so as to exactly cancel the repulsion between two electrons or two protons. The argument connecting these facts to the resulting attraction is not simple, but a kind of summary of it could be incorporated in the explanation of the attraction between surplus and deficit. Similarly, the transport of electrons from sweater to balloon could be explained in more depth.

Generating shallower explanations from a given set of rules may be more difficult, since in the current approach explanations are generated by the rules acting independently. Suppose one wanted to replace the explanations provided by three rules acting in sequence by a single, higher-level description. One would have to suppress the descriptions that some of the rules would produce on their own, and modify what would be produced by others. It might be simpler to introduce a hierarchy of rules, so that there is an explicit representation of a mechanism that summarizes the action of lower level rules, and then controls the level of rules that are allowed to describe themselves.

A third potential advantage of the amodal representation comes from its modularity, that is, that the rules that describe different mechanisms are largely independent. Because of this it may be easy to create related, but different, simulations. This would be done by reusing some of the rules from one simulation, and adding others, so as to describe a related situation.

This advantage was illustrated to some extent during the creation of the example program. The simulation involving just the sweater and the balloon was written first, and then the portion involving the wall was added. Three rules had to be added. But there was one only change needed to the existing rules, to establish that the attraction of the balloon to the wall, when it is placed there, is stronger than the attraction of the sweater.

Easy creation of related simulations may have pedagogical value. As discussed earlier, it seems important to support learners in identifying the mechanisms at work in a situation, and (if the mechanisms aren't described explicitly) this means identifying their conditions and actions from exploring different situations in which they are or are not in play. For example, if a condition for a mechanism is always satisfied in a simulation, one has no chance to see what the condition is. Similarly, if a condition is only satisfied in one way, its actual generality is obscure. Allowing learners to explore a family of simulations, with common mechanisms, may be useful.

Daniel Levin (personal communication, Bremen, June 8, 2017) suggests one more potential advantage of the amodal approach. Since the mechanisms involved in a simulation are represented explicitly, it may be possible to derive assessment items from them in a principled way. For example, one could describe a situation in which the conditions of a mechanism are or are not satisfied, and ask what would result, or ask under what conditions a specified event would occur.

This idea could be combined with the prospect of easier creation of simulations to support assessment via manipulation of a related simulation. For example, a learner could be asked to create an electron surplus on a rubber ball rather than on a balloon, or to use a rubber ball and a woolen scarf to rotate the dipoles in the wall.

Such examples have the desirable effect of pushing the representation of mechanisms toward greater generality. The current amodal simulation does not represent the fact that the balloon is made of rubber, and the sweater is made of wool, but it should.

How general is the amodal approach illustrated by our static electricity example? Not very, in its present form, as measured against the current collection of PhET simulations. As discussed earlier, most of the simulations are more quantitative in character, while the rules in our example are entirely qualitative. Extension to quantitative simulations seems possible, but remains to be explored. One would need quantitative mechanisms, that is, ones for which quantitative data are maintained as the simulation runs, conditions can test quantitative conditions, and actions can have quantitative effects. This in itself should not be difficult.

More challenging is providing good descriptions of the actions of the mechanisms, as are needed for the spoken descriptions in the example. It seems desirable that these descriptions, even for quantitative mechanisms, should be qualitative, as in, "When the charges move farther apart the attraction decreases," rather than "A distance of .75 cm produces an attraction of 5.2 N." It may be possible to bundle together the specification of the calculation for a mechanism with qualitative descriptions of some of its effects.

CHAPTER 5

Non-visual Visual Programming I: Dataflow

Following a conference panel presentation about inclusive design, a blind programmer in the audience called for the development of programming tools adapted for use by people with disabilities, so that they themselves can create and shape software for their own use. One of the panelists responded enthusiastically to this valuable idea. His response included a reference to the great progress in creating visual programming systems for end users, forgetting that visual programming would not be helpful for blind people.

This exchange might just seem careless. But it raises a good question: can the progress in visual programming for end users actually be exploited for blind people as well as sighted? The thinking of the distinguished blind computer scientist T V Raman, whom we met in the last chapter, suggests it can. Raman has suggested that the visual system can be thought of as the means by which sighted people ask and answer queries against a spatial database, that is, the visual world. If one has other means of managing the queries that are needed for an activity, one does not need the visual system (Raman, 1996; Raman and Gries, 1997; see also Lewis, 2013). This conception fits well within the framework of the theory of representations: instead of mapping a target domain to a representation domain that requires vision, one maps to a different representation domain, one that does not require vision. So allowing blind users to get the benefits that visual programming languages are thought to convey requires mapping the conceptual structure of such programs to a domain that does not require visual operations.

5.1 DATAFLOW PROGRAMMING

One popular form of visual programming supports computation considered as a collection of computational units connected by data paths that convey the results of one unit to another. Because of the conception of data flowing along these paths, this is called *dataflow* programming. Popular examples include LabView, used originally for controlling laboratory instruments, but now used for a wide range of applications, including interactive simulations (http://www.ni.com/en-us/shop/labview.html), and Max, used for music synthesis and video processing (https://cycling74.com/products/max/).

What are the benefits of dataflow languages that one would aim to maintain in a non-visual representation? While few or no good formal data are available on this, designers of these systems have offered some thoughts. One important theme is more natural support for parallelism than in conventional procedural languages. For example, National Instruments, developer of LabView and other dataflow systems, features this advantage in a white paper (http://www.ni.com/white-paper/6098/en/). The sequential nature of procedural code requires one to specify a serial order of execution for the statements in a program, even when the operations the statements specify could be performed in parallel. In a dataflow language one need only express the constraints that are forced by data dependencies: one cannot carry out a computation before its input data have been computed. If data are available for more than one computation, these computations can be carried out in parallel.

How this advantage translates into benefit for end user programmers isn't very clear, in general. However, in one class of situation there's a plausible argument. Suppose a user knows about a collection of things, each of which can autonomously carry out some operation, taking in some inputs and producing one or more outputs. Let's call the things "operators." And suppose that the user wants to accomplish some composite task that involves more than one of these operators working together, with the outputs from some being the inputs to others. Then it seems that dataflow is the simplest way of specifying the composite. All one must do is specify what outputs are to be connected to what inputs, an unavoidable requirement.

In the case of LabView, the core of the language supports a collection of operators that includes measurement instruments and signal generators that can be connected to things in the world, outside the system, and operators that transform and combine the kinds of signals the measurement instruments produce. This allows end users to create and operate flexible measurement instruments for particular purposes.

Another domain in which dataflow languages are popular is electronic music. Here operators are provided that can be connected to a speaker, to produce sound, or to a microphone to capture sound. Further operators transform or combine representations of sounds within the system, for example making a sound louder or softer, changing its pitch, or adding two sounds together, as in a chord. Max (https://cycling74.com/) and Pure Data (https://puredata.info/) are popular examples of systems of this kind.

PuppyIR (Azzopardi, et al. 2009) aims to support the flexible development of information services for children, using a dataflow framework to connect operators that access online services, such as Youtube, to operators that produce presentations on information, via operators that transform or combine information. Much earlier, Show and Tell (Kimura et al., 1986) proposed a dataflow-based system for home information systems.

Reflecting on the common inspiration for these systems, then, one can suggest that a key conceptual advantage of dataflow is a kind of minimality. Data dependencies must be specified in a computational system, and in a dataflow language one doesn't have to specify anything else. Other kinds of languages introduce features outside this minimum, which then must be understood.

In their presentation of Show and Tell, Kimura et al. (1986) argue for a further advantage of dataflow that they term *keyboardless programming*. They note that creating something by combining characters, as is required in textual languages, can be difficult for some users, such as young children. They note that a dataflow system, with its collection of operators, lends itself to programming by selecting operators from a layout rather than by typing names. The selected operators are then connected by data paths that express the data dependencies.

Collecting these ideas, the conceptual essence of a dataflow language is the selection of operators from a collection of available ones, and the ability to specify connections between inputs and outputs on the selected operators. Since programs must be read, as well as written, a design has to consider how operators and connections between them can be discovered in a completed program.

5.2 NOODLE: NON-VISUAL DATAFLOW

Figure 5.1 shows examples of a dataflow programs presented visually. It's clear that a key operation in understanding a dataflow program is tracing the data paths. Where does the input to this operation come from? What happens next to this result? Such questions are answered by tracing the data paths that provide inputs to, or dispatch outputs from, a computational unit.

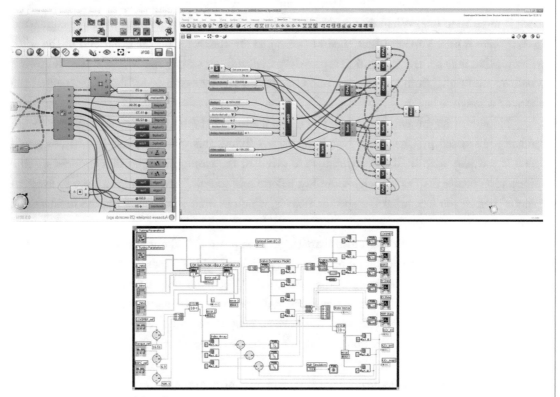

Figure 5.1: Examples of dataflow programs.

The program Noodle (Lewis, 2014) shows how the same conceptual structure can be managed without visual operations. Like any dataflow program, a Noodle program consists of operators interconnected by data paths. In Noodle these paths connect to input or output connectors on the operators; these connectors are named. The user can step through the connectors on an operator, using keyboard commands; the name of each connector is read out, so that the user can identify the desired one. Having thus navigated to a connector, the user can trace the data path using an additional keyboard command, arriving at the connector on the other end of the path.

One can note that in some ways this non-visual operation is easier than the corresponding visual operation in visual presentations of dataflow programs. As is suggested by the examples in Figure 5.1, it is not always easy to trace a data path, as it may cross over or under other paths, or may run alongside another path for a stretch, sometimes requiring careful attention to follow. The non-visual operation in Noodle reliably traverses any path in a way unaffected by other paths.

Specifically, this is done using *pseudospatial navigation*, somewhat like that used in the menu structure for the electric field simulation described in Chapter 2. Noodle presents a palette of operators, conceptually at the "left" side of the screen, and a workspace to the "right." When visiting an operator in the workspace, moving to the "right" (using the right arrow key) takes one onto the first connector that the operator has. Moving "up" or "down" moves one among these connectors, if there is more than one. When on a connector, moving "right" takes one onto the edge connected to it, if there is one. Moving "right" again takes on to the connector on the other end of the edge, wherever that may be. This navigation is pseudospatial, and not simply spatial, since after following a path to the "right" from an operator, one ends up on an element that is "above" or "below" the operator where one began.

Noodle in its present form gives you a chance to feel the impact of Sina Bahram's design guidance, discussed in Chapter 2. Noodle does not follow this guidance, and it hurts, as you'll know if you play with it. The descriptions are given in the wrong order, so that the less specific information comes first, as in "palette amplify, palette mix sounds," and so on: you have to listen to "palette" before you hear what the specific item is, which is what you need. Also, the menus don't wrap around, so you hang up at the ends if you try to move quickly.

The current Noodle design also worries perhaps too much about keeping you oriented as you navigate. Suppose you are on an operator in the palette, and you then perform an action, such as inserting a copy of the operator in the workspace. When you now ask to move along to another palette item, the interface does not move you when you first press the arrow key, but rather keeps you where you are, and tells you. You have to press the arrow key again to move. The idea is to make sure you know where you are, but it's probably the wrong tradeoff, as it slows down an already slow process.

In its current form Noodle does not support any control of the layout of operators. It is plausible that grouping related operators together spatially makes it easier for users to grasp the overall structure of a program. If this proves true, it would be possible to add controls for this to Noodle, allowing navigation in two dimensions within programs, though some change would be needed to distinguish moving to the right from an operator to another one, within the invisible layout of a program, from moving to right from an operator onto its list of connectors. For example, a selection operation could be added to signal the latter operation.

The limited proof of concept implementation of Noodle supports a few very simple operations on sounds, and (without non-visual support for viewing the results) some simple graphics.

5.3   REFLECTION

Does Noodle represent a viable approach to a non-visual programming system for end users? Leaving aside the clunkiness of its crude interaction design, which could certainly be improved greatly, there are issues to consider. One is the value of the keyboardless programming paradigm, in which programs are constructed by selection and connection, rather than by typing. For many blind people, typing, and reading text with a screen reader, are well-developed skills. Such users may be better served by systems that capitalize on these skills. For example, Andy Stefik's Quorum system (https://quorumlanguage.com/) is a powerful textual language specifically designed for ease of use with a screen reader (while also having advantages for sighted users, as shown in empirical studies).

On the other hand, the repeated emergence of dataflow as a programming model suggests that the conceptual minimality of dataflow may be a significant advantage, in some application domains. Might this advantage be captured in a typing-based language? Likely it could, perhaps using names for data paths, together with a navigation aid for quickly moving from one end of a path to the other.

Finally, there's a further potential benefit of non-visual keyboardless programming to be weighed. Typing is difficult on small devices like smartphones, but their limited screen size makes conventional visual presentation of keyboardless programming difficult. Could an evolved version of Noodle support workable keyboardless programming on phones?

CHAPTER 6

Non-visual Visual Programming II: A Blocks Language

A popular way to introduce programming to children is with *blocks languages*, of which Scratch (scratch.mit.edu) is the most popular example. In a blocks language, programs are built up not from text but from blocks, colored shapes, as shown in Figure 6.1. This is another instance of the keyboardless programming paradigm: the shapes are chosen from a layout, and then assembled.

The point of this block representation is that syntactic constraints in a textual language are replaced by *shape* constraints: the shape of a block indicates the contexts in which it can be placed. Tabs and sockets must match. Users are freed from the frustrations of misplaced parentheses or semicolons making programs inoperable. A program whose blocks can be fit together will always be syntactically correct (though of course it may not do what its creator wants.) Continuing to follow T. V. Raman's thinking, as in the last chapter, how can the conceptual structure of a blocks language be supported by a non-visual presentation?

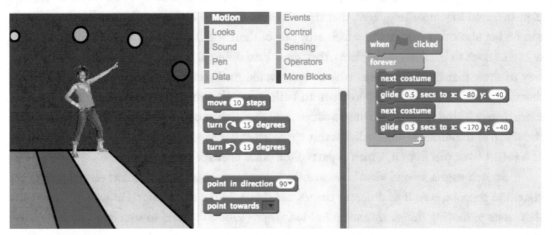

Figure 6.1: A Scratch program.

Pseudospatial Blocks (program PB; Koushik and Lewis, 2016a, 2016b) illustrates one approach. As in Noodle, visual presentation of a toolbox of program, and a workspace containing blocks that form a program, is replaced by an arrangement of elements in an invisible space, navigated using arrow keys. The navigational scheme is a bit more complex than that for Noodle, because blocks can be nested, for example in loop or conditional constructions. Broadly, chains of blocks that represent sequences of actions are arranged vertically. To move among the parts of a block that represent its operands, for example two expressions to be added, or a number of repetitions, and a nested sequence of statements to be repeated, for a loop construction, one moves horizontally. To navigate one of these parts one must first select it; the arrow keys then navigate within the selected part.

This navigation scheme, like that of Noodle, is pseudospatial. For example, when moving down within a sequence of blocks one wraps around at the bottom, so that by moving down repeatedly one finds oneself at the top of a sequence (see discussion of the Bahram guidelines in Chapter 2). Similarly, moving to the right or left from a part of a block on may find that one has moved to the top of the adjoining part, not into the middle, as faithful spatiality would require.

As mentioned earlier, a key feature of blocks languages is the replacement of syntactic constraints by shape matching. How can this visual operation be performed non-visually? The required effects are that it should be clear what program elements will fit in a given location in a program, and that an element cannot be placed in a place where it doesn't fit. Both of these effects are accomplished in PB by the use of *filtering*. To add an element to a PB program one first selects the place in the program where one intends to place it. The available program elements are then filtered so that only the elements that can legally be placed in that position are offered for selection.

Arguably, filtering has advantages over shape matching beyond being more inclusive. It often happens, even in simple languages, that there are contexts in which two different kinds of blocks can fit, but also other contexts in which only one of those kinds will fit. Given that the two kinds of blocks don't fit in all the same places, they must have different shapes. But then there's no simple way to show that there are places where either would fit. Vasek (2012) and Lerner et al. (2015) describe partial solutions to this problem. In both approaches there are visual cues that show that more than one kind of block will fit in a socket, and then (when one of the kinds is actually in place) the shape of the socket is adjusted. But this approach still means that you can't tell from the shape of a socket what will fit in it, which is part of the point of shape coding.

Scratch uses a second visual cue to help in program construction, color: elements that are related in purpose, even if of different shapes, are shown in the same color. For example, elements that relate to moving things are shown in blue, while elements related to sound are shown in magenta. PB uses named groups of elements to replace this use of colors. Elements in the toolbox are assigned to categories, each with a name. These names are read as one navigates within the toolbox, making it easier to find a desired element.

The implementation of PB uses declarative specification of the effect of keyboard commands. This is intended to make it easier to explore variations in navigation. For example, in the current navigation scheme, if one is navigating a sequence of statements, and reaches a loop, one navigates directly into the body of the loop, without requiring a selection operation. This choice is based on the presumption that this is the common case, and that work is eased by not requiring the selection. But this may be confusing, since selection is required in other similar situations, for example involving expressions. The declarative specification should make it easy to explore such choices.

PB might be modified to support other classes of users: those who can see, but cannot use a mouse, and (in fact) those who cannot use a conventional keyboard. PB's ability to operate using only keyboard commands—called keyboard accessibility—means that using a mouse is not necessary. It also means that someone who can't use an ordinary keyboard can use assistive technology that converts head movements, eye gaze, or other inputs into signals that emulate a keyboard. For sighted users PB should produce visual representations of the toolbox and the workspace, which it does not do now.

Box: 6.1

Other Approaches to Making Blocks Languages Accessible

A number of other groups are working on making blocks languages more accessible, and PB is thus just one in a large space of possibilities to explore. Other efforts include those of Ludi (2015) and Milne (2017). Milne's work is especially notable because it uses visual presentation on a touchscreen to support users with vision as well as those without. A great many people have some vision, and make use of what they have, rather than working with purely non-visual presentations. Supporting this audience is an important design challenge, as discussed by Szpiro et al. (2016).

PB uses Blockly, a library developed by Google to support implementation of blocks languages (Fraser, 2015), and the Blockly group has created Accessible Blockly (https://blockly-demo.appspot.com/static/demos/accessible/index.html) to address the need. Accessible Blockly is screen reader based, relying on users being familiar with how to navigate a hierarchy using screen reader commands.

It's an interesting question whether this hierarchical approach is best for learners generally. As just mentioned, PB departs from the hierarchical structure of blocks code when navigating a sequence of statements: in PB, the statement block that follows a repeat statement is the first statement in the body of the repeat, not the next statement in the program after the repeat. This choice reflects the notion that when trying to understand code it's not very helpful to know that there is a repeat statement without hearing right away what it is that's being repeated. Strict hierarchy requires using a different operation to read the body of the repeat; one can't just step through the code.

Another issue, quite complex, is whether reliance on screen reader skills is generally a good idea or not, for various audiences. On the one hand, skilled screen reader users benefit from interfaces that support their skills, and it can be very uncomfortable when an interface does not support them. On the other hand, by no means all people who don't see well are screen reader users. They may find pseudospatial navigation as in PB simpler. On the third hand, perhaps encouraging learners to develop screen reader skills is strategically better than encouraging them to do without. A lot of evolution will likely be needed to find a reasonable resolution of these dilemmas.

To relate the issues to our representational framework, we can see that effectiveness for screen reader users is different from effectiveness for non screen reader users, with the added complication that a non screen reader user could turn into a screen reader user.

An exciting effort, that provides flexible screen reader support, and has the benefit of Sina Bahram's design insights (along with those of the project team, led by Emanuel Schanzer), is Bootstrap, the platform for a program that integrates math learning and programming (http://www.bootstrapworld.org/). It offers a block representation of programs, though not one that uses shape coding (all blocks are the same shape), and so may not offer all the benefits of other block language designs.

Bootstrap supports *functional* programming, which means that the problem of navigating sequential code, of the kind that is universal in what are called *procedural* languages, like Scratch, doesn't come up. All programs have more or less the same kind of tree structure, the kind that shows up in mathematical expressions, while procedural programs mix those with another kind that's appropriate to sequences. It's that difference that leads PB to do funny things with hierarchical structure.

The Bootstrap team is making great progress in providing good navigation for their expression structures, including the tough problem of navigating structures that have mistakes in them. You can follow their progress in their blog at http://www.bootstrap-world.org/blog/index.shtml.

Ever since functional programming was invented there have been those who argue that it is fundamentally better than procedural programs, and more who hotly reject that assertion. Current use favors procedural programming by a wide margin. It will be interesting if better support for inclusive design for learners plays a role in shifting that balance.

6.1 NON-VISUAL PROGRAMMING TASKS

A popular space of tasks for children learning to program is turtle graphics (developed by Seymour Papert and colleagues as part of the LOGO language project; Papert, 1971). As discussed further in Chapter 7, turtle graphics supports learners creating geometrical patterns by issuing commands that make a real or virtual robot move forward specified distances, or turn through specified angles, while leaving a visible trace. Also popular today are activities in which learners create animations. But what about children who can't see the graphics?

The Bootstrap project, already mentioned, is breaking new ground here, in harnessing machine vision technology to produce descriptions of graphical patterns, along with other techniques for producing spoken descriptions of the graphical output of programs; see blog post at http://www. bootstrapworld.org/blog/accessibility/Describing-Images-Screenreaders.shtml.

A possible alternative, addressed in PB, is replacing these visually oriented activities with ones oriented toward sound. PB supports simple operations on musical notes, of two kinds. In *direct play*, a note block makes a sound when executed; in *indirect play*, a note block creates a representation of a sound that can be transformed before it is played, by a separate operation.

Arguably, indirect play supports a richer space of operations, more naturally. In particular, one can create chords by combining two or more sounds before playing them. On the other hand, direct play shows sequences of notes more simply: blocks for the desired notes are simply fitted together in order, while sounds in indirect play have to be concatenated before playing them. This may make sequences somewhat harder to understand, as creating a sequence in indirect play is more complex, involving explicit concatenation operations, and, by itself, doesn't seem to "do" anything.

More generally, the production of music as an arena for learning to program seems to have interesting strengths and weaknesses. Repetition arises naturally, as well as other operations on sequences. But conditionals don't seem natural to the domain, or function definition; standard musical notion includes neither. This doesn't mean, however, that such constructs could not usefully be included in a language supporting exploration of music; see, for example, Shapiro et al., 2016.

CHAPTER   7

Auditory Turtle Graphics

As mentioned in the previous chapter, a popular way to introduce some programming concepts, and to support an understanding of some concepts in geometry, is turtle graphics. Here one creates geometric forms by commanding a "turtle" (these days almost always a cursor on a display, but originally a small robot that somewhat resembled a turtle) to move ahead, or to turn, while leaving a trace of its motion. For example, the turtle can draw an equilateral triangle with side 10 by moving ahead 10 steps, turning right 120°, moving ahead 10 steps, turning right 120°, and moving ahead 10 steps (and turning 120° again, to return to one's starting configuration.) Turtle graphics systems include various other commands, for example to repeat a group of commands. Using a repeat command the triangle could be expressed as "repeat 3 times: ahead 10, right 120"; a square can be drawn by "repeat 4 times: ahead 10, right 90," and so on. In the popular Scratch system, discussed in the previous chapter, any "sprite," a picture shown on the screen, can be made to act like a turtle.

For children who can watch the turtle, and observe the patterns it makes, turtle graphics can be informative, and fun. Various extensions are possible; Mike Eisenberg and collaborators have devised turtle graphics on a sphere, so that one can explore a world in which the sum of the angles in a triangle isn't 180°, but depends on the size of the triangle, and in which moving in a fixed direction does not trace a shortest path between points, in general (Eisenberg et al., 2013).

But what if you can't see? A natural experiment is to replace the visible turtle by an invisible one that makes a sound as it moves. Can one localize the turtle well enough from its sounds, so as to grasp how it is responding to commands, and what forms it makes? To assess effectiveness, one could ask hearers to identify an equilateral triangle, or (with more ambition) a five-pointed star.

Working with synthetic sounds one can use spatialized sound (supported in the Web Audio API supported by most browsers) to generate stereo sound that "originates" from any desired location, say in a plane in front of the listener. The reader can experiment with this idea with the program Turtle. If you do, it will be more interesting if you don't know what shapes are "drawn" by the buttons in the program, so don't read the legend in Table 7.1 until you have tried the program.

Button	Shape
Shape 1	Triangle
Shape 2	square
Shape 3	star
Shape 4	circle
Shape 5	spiral

Table 7.1: Shapes associated with the buttons in the Turtle program

To my ear, the precision of localization is nowhere near good enough to pass the suggested assessments.

This shouldn't be surprising. While accuracy in identifying the source of a sound along the left-right axis is quite good, determining how high up a sound source is, or how far away it is, is difficult. So, we can try mapping the vertical axis, or if we prefer an "away" axis of our auditory display, to frequency, something people are well able to discriminate. The reader can try this with the program TurtleFreq. Unfortunately here, too, my ear can't determine the geometry of the turtle's movements well enough to pass.

These simple experiments may not do justice to the possibilities for conveying geometry with some, however. In the next chapter we'll consider connections between music and movement in space. Keeping for now to simpler sounds, Albert Bregman, mentioned earlier as the founder of auditory scene analysis, the science of the interpretation of sound by people, suggests that we are neglecting powerful cues to geometry: the way sounds change when one moves one's head, or moves one's whole body so as to observe how a sound changes as our position relative to it, and to reflectors and absorbers in the environment, changes (Bregman, 2014). Unfortunately, these matters can't be explored with synthetic sounds just with simple headphones or speakers, since such a system can't tell where the listener is, or the position of their head, relative to the simulated sound source, and so the sounds it generates can't change as they should.

Two responses to this limitation are possible. First, using an actual robotic turtle, as was done in the early days, a listener would have all the affordances Bregman notes: they can turn their head, or move about, and use the changes in what they hear as information about the position of the robot.

I mocked up a version of this, with a colleague as observer. I drew several shapes on a desk pad sheet: an equilateral triangle, a right triangle, a square, a regular pentagon, and a five-pointed star (see Figure 7.1). The lengths of the sides ranged from 5 to 12 inches. I asked my colleague to listen, eyes closed, as I traced a shape repeatedly, rubbing the handle of a spoon on the paper. They were free to move around the table where I was tracing, and to move their head as they wished.

What could they hear? They were able to report the number of parts of the figures, and when the lengths of the parts were the same or different, and that there were angles rather than curves, but did not give names to any of the forms. That is, something with three equal parts was not identified as an equilateral triangle. The star was heard as "disorganized." After I showed them the paper with the figures drawn on it, we repeated the exercise. They were able to identify the right triangle, the square, and the regular pentagon. Interestingly, they did not identify the equilateral triangle: they said they had not noticed it when looking at the paper. So whatever impression of shape the tracing provided was not sufficient to identify an equilateral triangle without the benefit of specific knowledge of it as an alternative. Similarly, when I traced a square somewhat smaller than the one drawn on the paper it was not heard as a square, but as (without much confidence) the star.

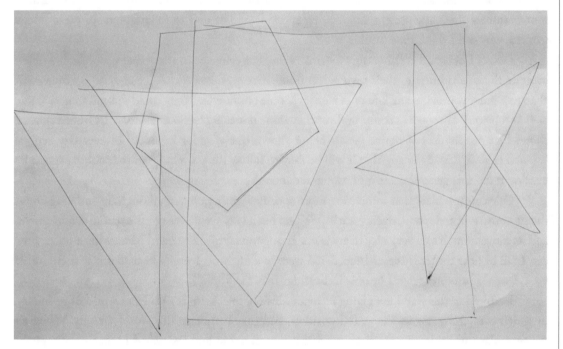

Figure 7.1: Figures traced to test auditory shape detection.

Much more could be explored in this paradigm. For example, the sound made by the spoon handle on the paper may be more difficult to localize than some other sound. Perhaps using somewhat larger shapes could help. But on their own the added affordances of head and body movement are not sufficient to convey good information about even rather simple and regular shapes.

A second possibility stays in the realm of synthetic sound, and headphones, but uses head tracking to inform the sound system where the listener is, and how their head is oriented. The sound system can then modify the sound sent to the headphones so as to correspond to what they should hear, in their virtual position. I'm not optimistic about the potential here, given the negative results just described for physical movement of a sound source. But the synthetic approach offers some additional possibilities, including exaggerating stereo and distance effects, that may aid localization. Perhaps a properly equipped reader will explore these possibilities.

7.1   THE MYTH OF GEOMETRY

I was optimistic about all of the failed explorations in this chapter. Even though I had read that the cues for auditory localization are uncertain, especially for distance away from the hearer, I was confident that synthetic stereo sound would allow me to hear simple shapes. Or that substituting frequency for loudness as a cue for distance or height would work. Or, surely, that the rubbing sounds from a physically present and moving spoon would be easy to follow. None of these things worked; why did I think they would?

Daniel Levin and collaborators marshal a mass of evidence to show that people consistently overrate the effectiveness of their own perception (see, e.g., Levin and Angelone, 2008). Studies of change blindness provide one line of evidence: people are sure that they could not fail to notice this or that "obvious" change in a scene, and yet they don't notice it (Levin et al., 2000). Other evidence shows that people do not notice events being shown out of order in videos of everyday actions (Hymel et al., 2016). Believing that it will be easy to follow the movement of the rubbing spoon by hearing it fits this general pattern of overconfidence.

One can speculate that something more specific is going on here, though. In thinking about the movement of the spoon, tracing a triangle, one has a very vivid sense of the spatial arrangement, and its movement: it's all very easy to envision. The spoon is right *there*, and it's making a noise; how can I fail to hear that it is there? Indeed, if I were looking at it, I *would* hear that it is there (or, at least, I would interpret what I hear as indicating that it is "there").

In thinking this way I am giving in to an illusion, that there is a uniform world of geometry, in which everything has its shape and position, and that I perceive this world directly. When all my senses are available, the gap between this mythical world and the world I perceive often goes unnoticed. Indeed, the coordination of sensation is such as to support the illusion. But even under these conditions, demonstrations like change blindness show that there are actually enormous discrepancies between what is actually present and what I perceive.

When I ask myself what I will notice, in a change blindness study, I imagine the "objective" geometry of the scene I'll be shown, and its possible changes. I imagine myself perceiving that scene, and the myth tells me that my perception simply makes all that geometry, and its dynamics, available to me. But it does not. Instead, my perception results in what I interpret as definite geometry, and dynamics, that turn out to be sharply different from the "reality": I miss "obvious" changes. Unavailable to my reflection is the actually fragmentary nature of what I pick up from the scene, on the basis of which my constructed perception of it is formed.

When some sensory information is unavailable, the discrepancies expand, but the picture I have of my own perception does not change. I can still picture that concrete geometry: there's the shape, there's the spoon, there I am hearing it. But I don't realize that the information needed to determine the geometry is no longer available to me, through hearing alone.

Susanna Millar (1994) discusses these matters in her book, *Understanding and Representing Space: Theory and Evidence from Studies with Blind and Sighted Children*. She notes other situations in which the myth of geometry breaks down. For example, many people have supposed that small three-dimensional models of objects would be easy to recognize by touch. After all, such a model has a definite shape, that can be pictured vividly; how could running the fingers over the model fail to reveal its shape? But Millar notes that the actual information available from touching a small object is different, and is obtained differently, from the information gained from exploring large objects. In fact, Millar argues that recognizing shapes by touch differs for six different classes of tactual shapes (p. 91), differences just not relevant, or even conceivable, in the world of geometry we think of ourselves as inhabiting. Children need help in learning how the information they obtain from a small object relates to information they obtain about large ones.

Millar derives specific practical suggestions from her analysis: one should provide cues from body and hand movement to replace visual information, when it is missing (Millar, 1994, p. 257). Thus, a kinesthetic turtle, one whose movements are followed with the hand, might be superior to an auditory one. Can you create one?

Another possibility, suggested by Millar's work, is that experience in working with particular combinations of cues will lead to improvements in interpreting them. My sighted colleague and I can't perceive the location of the spoon; perhaps a blind person, who has a great deal of experience working with the relevant cues, could do so.

CHAPTER 8

Music and Movement: Truslit

Some music gives some listeners a vivid impression of movement in space. Can these impressions be used to convey spatial information, perhaps of the sort discussed in Chapter 2 on the dynamic structure of an electric field? There we were interested in trying to convey shapes like circles and spirals, with auditory representations.

Promising results can be glimpsed in the work of Alexander Truslit, for example in Figure 8.1. The columns of the figure show short musical passages, accompanied by pictorial renderings of spatial forms associated with them. One participant first conceived of a motion, as drawn in the second column, and then created music to go with it, as shown in the first column. These scores were then given to a second participant, who drew the spatial forms suggested by the music, shown in the third column. While the original spatial forms and those recovered from the music are not identical in all cases, the similarities are certainly strong enough to be intriguing.

Truslit's work was published in 1938, just before World War II, in Germany, and dropped from sight. Bruno Repp (1993a) rediscovered it, and published a synopsis and partial translation, in 1993, from which Figure 8.1 is taken. Sadly, by this time Truslit was presumed dead; anyway, there are gaps in what can be recovered about Truslit's methods. The participants were "both well versed in the methods described in this book," but just what that means, and what kind of training was involved, isn't known. Repp speculates that the second participant may have been Truslit himself.

These methodological uncertainties matter when we assess the meaning, and potential usefulness, of Truslit's results. What we would most want would be a way to communicate different curves using musical sound, for untrained users. But if we assume, as seems likely, that Truslit's participants were extensively trained, they might have learned to use a set of *conventions* that allowed each of them to associate sounds and curves. Each might be trained to draw a particular kind of curve to represent a particular figure in a melody (and to associate the melody to that curve). There might be little or nothing that the sounds would communicate about curves to untrained participants, and little or nothing to guide an untrained participant who has to create a melody to represent a given curve. Such a training-dependent system of correspondence might perhaps have some utility, but only in a setting in which it would be worth investing in the representational conventions for some class of curves.

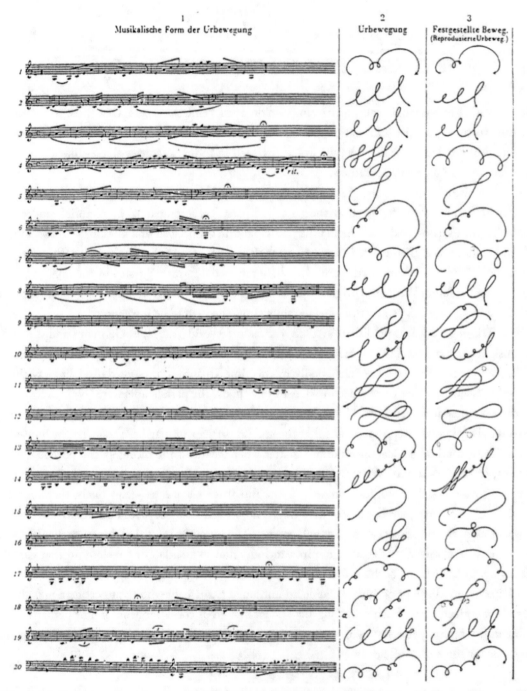

Figure 8.1: Experiment on the recovery of original motion from notated music. (1) Examples notated by subject N. (2) Original motion curves, as drawn by subject N. (3) Motion curves drawn by subject T. Figure and caption reproduced from Repp (1993a), used with permission.

But perhaps the associations between sounds and curves are not just conventional. In an historical review of work on motion in music, Repp (1993b) suggests that these curved forms are natural responses to the imagined movement of a sort of cursor, with higher pitches heard as the cursor being spatially high, and lower pitches suggesting that the cursor is spatially low. Referring to work on the kinematics of hand movements by Viviani and colleagues (Viviani and Terzuolo, 1982; Viviani and Cenzato, 1985; Viviani and Schneider, 1991), Repp suggests that the rate of change of pitch conveys the speed of motion of the cursor, and that acceleration or deceleration convey a sense of curvature: something making a tight turn has to slow down, while a gentle curve can be taken at speed.

A striking feature of Truslit's curves is their cyclic character, including retrograde motion: the cursor doesn't just move off to the right (say), moving up and down as the pitch does, but circles back, and sometimes moves back and forth as it moves up and down. This aspect of Truslit's conception is appealing to me, as I sometimes have the sense, when listening, of music swinging back and forth, and sometimes making a full circle, and sometimes reversing the direction of apparent rotation.

So I've attempted to reproduce the impressions of movement in Truslit's diagrams, with partial, but only partial, success. The program TruslitExamples plays two of the scores, numbers 3 and 4, from Truslit's Figure 3, shown above as Figure 8.1. It will also play six other examples, from another of Truslit's figures, shown in Figure 8.2.

 Unfortunately, the quality of the reproduction of the musical notation in the original is poor, and I can't be sure that I have read them with complete accuracy. But the program perhaps gives some sense of what Truslit's listeners heard.

Readers can form their own impressions of these musical passages. The clearest feeling of hearing what Truslit heard came for me with examples 5 and 6, in which I felt the presence of a smaller loop within a larger one, in 6 but not in 5, in agreement with Truslit. But I don't hear Truslit's figure eight movement in either example.

To explore this matter further, I created another program, TruslitSandbox, with which to explore the space of movements suggested by periodic sequences of notes. I was able to produce (to my ear) some of the effects Truslit seems to have heard.

The program allows you to try out all kinds of things, with different notes, lengths, and loudness, and to compare two different note sequences, but it can be a bit tedious to set up. So it also has buttons that play some preset examples, at the very bottom of the screen. The button Preset 1 plays two versions of the same six notes, repeated a few times, but with different timings. To my ear, the first of the two sequences sounds like a rotation, but interrupted each time around, rather than smooth, while the second sequence sounds as if it swings back and forth, rather than rotating. The contrast between the two perhaps gets at some of the complexity that Truslit heard.

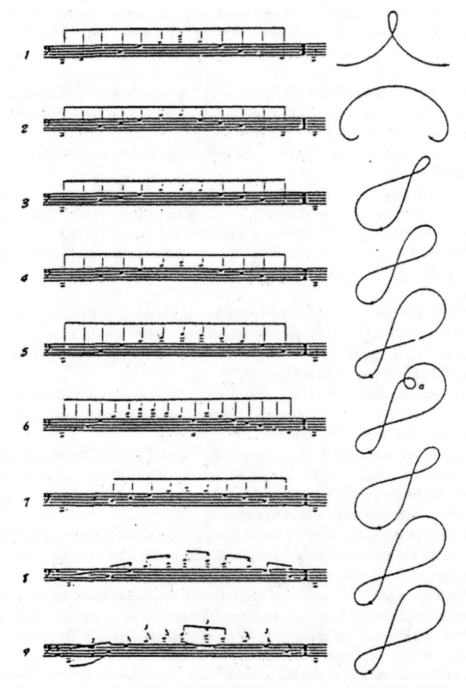

Figure 8.2: Musical scores on the left, and graphical forms associated with each, on the right.

A specific suggestion that Truslit makes, clarified by Repp, is that apparent radius of curvature is related to the speed of pitch changes, as just mentioned. Motion has to slow down to round a tight turn. Preset 2 explores this. To my ear, both sequences move around a circle, but the first makes a smaller circle than the second.

There are two differences between these sequences. The first sequence covers a smaller range of pitches than second, and also is played faster. Preset 3 compares the same sequence of notes, played faster and then slower. To my ear, the second still makes a larger circle, even though the range of notes is the same. In fact, the first sequence sounds less round, as would be expected from the idea that faster motion means less curvature.

If the reader wants to experiment with these sequences in the program, they can be set up using the information in Table 8.1, and then modified. Each Preset compares two sequences, so two sequences of notes and lengths are shown for each. Notes can be added or removed by setting the corresponding lengths to zero or nonzero values, so the program can handle two sequences of up to 20 notes.

Table 8.1: Parameters for the presets in TruslitSandbox						
Preset 1						
notes	G3	B3	D4	F4	D4	B3
lengths	250	250	500	250	250	500
notes	G3	B3	D4	F4	D4	B3
lengths	250	500	250	250	500	250
Preset 2						
notes	G3	B3	D4	F4	D4	B3
lengths	250	250	250	250	250	250
notes	E3	G3	F#4	A4	F#4	G3
lengths	350	350	350	350	350	350
Preset 3						
notes	E3	G3	F#4	A4	F#4	G3
lengths	250	250	250	250	250	250
notes	E3	G3	F#4	A4	F#4	G3
lengths	350	350	350	350	350	350

A high-level impression is that this is an interesting space, but also very large: I've only scratched the surface of the possibilities that could be investigated, which would include, to mention just one unexplored variable, harmonic relationships, either between notes in a single voice, or between notes in chords. For that matter, even though TruslitSandbox supports it, I've not explored differences in loudness, at all. Truslit suggests that loudness is indeed important. Perhaps the wider range of impressions Truslit reports could be captured in other regions of this space. Perhaps the reader will find some.

However that may be, the impression of cyclic motion, on different radii, could be enough to serve some representational purposes. Remembering the problem of conveying the holistic pattern of field propagation, in Chapter 2, we could consider whether Truslit motions could be used to provide an approach. Could one play a sequence of sequences, giving the impression of circles of increasing size, to convey the geometry of expanding rings of disturbance, as when a pebble is dropped in a pool? And could one instead make the radius change during a cycle, so as to depict the spiral form that the disturbance actually shows, in contrast to the rings in the pool?

The reader can listen to some attempts along these lines using the program TruslitCurves. This program differs from the previous ones in a few ways. For one thing, rather than playing discrete notes, it plays a continuous tone. Taking literally the idea of pitch being determined by the height of a kind of cursor, the program makes a cursor follow a curve, and sets the pitch from the height of the cursor, as it moves. Also following Truslit and Repp, the speed of the cursor along the curve depends on the curvature: a tighter turn means a slower cursor. (You can turn off this curvature effect in the program; if you do, the cursor moves at a constant speed along the curve, regardless of the curvature.) The program lets you listen to a series of circles, of increasing radius, or to a spiral. (It also lets you listen to some ellipses, whose curvature is greater in some places than others.)

To my ear, differences in radius are audible, as the rings play, but I can't distinguish the "spiral" depiction, with progressively increasing radii, from the rings. I don't think someone would get the idea of spiral spatial pattern by listening to these sounds. So I account this experiment in utility a failure. But perhaps readers will find Truslit's world intriguing, and explore it further. Truslit returns in Chapter 10, in an exploration of how his curves might provide a new way to create music, or a kind of music.

CHAPTER 9

Representing Higher-dimensional Structures

As we've been seeing, sound has representational potential that's not much explored. But visual representations also can do new things. In this chapter we'll explore representations too big to fit into the familiar world of three dimensions.

Many situations involve these big structures, ones with more than three dimensions, that are therefore challenging to present. This can happen because one wishes to show entities with more than three continuous quantitative attributes, that one wishes to represent as spatial dimensions. For example, one might want to display the weight, displacement, and gas mileage of a collection of automobiles; here, each car could be represented by a point in a three-dimensional space. But if one also wants to represent the price of the cars, an additional dimension would be needed.

Another common case is representing the dynamics of three-dimensional structures, that is, their changes over time. If one wishes to treat time as a spatial dimension (a choice we'll motivate below) one is again dealing with a structure with four dimensions.

How might one depict a structure of four or more spatial dimensions? The most common approach is to use *projection*: one maps points in four dimensions onto points in three dimensions. For example, one could simply map all points that differ only in the fourth dimension onto the same point in three dimensions. This yields a three-dimensional structure that can then be visualized in two dimensions (on a screen, for example) by a further projection.

Figure 9.1 shows this at work in viewing a four-dimensional wire frame cube. Leaving the cube in the simplest orientation, with the edges aligned with the coordinate axes, as shown in panel a, doesn't give a very interesting or informative picture, because many of the vertices and edges are lined up, and can't see seen. Rotating the cube can give the much more interesting view seen in panel b.

The wire frame is nice, but of course not solid. The wish naturally arises to show a solid cube. Here a problem arises with the projection method. Suppose we color the faces of the four-dimensional cube. What colors should be shown in the various areas in Figure 9.1b? Unfortunately, there's no straightforward answer to this question.

When projecting three dimensions down to two, the situation is clear. Corresponding to any point in the two-dimensional image there is a single ray in the three-dimensional space, containing all points that project to that image point. The points on a ray have a clear ordering: of any two distinct points in the ray, one must be closer, and that is the one that should be "seen," that is, its color should determine the color of the corresponding point in the image. When a four-dimensional space is being collapsed to a two-dimensional image, however, the collection of points in the space that are mapped to a given point in the image is a two-dimensional form. In a two-dimensional form there can be many points, all mapping to the same point in the image, and all equidistant from the image point. If they are of different colors, all the colors have equal claim to be chosen for the point in the image.

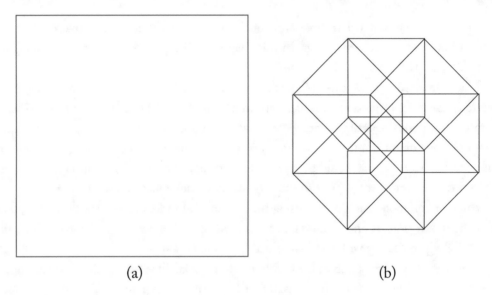

(a)   (b)

Figure 9.1: Two views of a four-dimensional wire-frame cube.

This problem can be avoided, by thinking differently about how the process of seeing in three dimensions can be generalized to seeing in four or more dimensions. Instead of projecting the entire space onto the image plane, one can instead stipulate that the apparatus of vision consists of a two-dimensional retina, on which the image will be formed, and a viewpoint, represented by single point distinct from the retina (see Figure 9.2). What is shown at a given point on the retina is determined by drawing a ray from the viewpoint through the point on the retina, and out into the space. What is seen is whatever that ray first hits.

It's easy to see that this solves the problem of what color to make the image points: there is always a unique closest point among all those that are mapped to a given point on the retina.

But this clarity comes at a cost. For any given position of the retina and viewpoint, only those points that fall within the bundle of rays running from the retina through the viewpoint, and no matter how big the space is, this bundle is always a structure of just three dimensions. Any points outside this three-dimensional region are simply invisible.

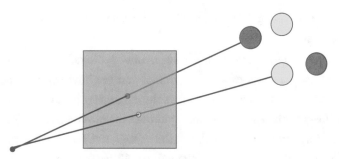

Figure 9.2: The color of a point on the retina is determined by the color of the first point along the ray that passes from the viewpoint through the point on the retina.

How could such a limited viewing arrangement possibly be workable? By moving the retina and viewpoint, any given point in the space, no matter how large the space is, can be brought into view. One might compare this to exploring a large, dark room with a small flashlight. For any one position of the flashlight one can see only a small part of the room. But one can explore the whole room by moving the light around.

These two viewing schemes, simple projection and the retina and viewpoint scheme, represent an interesting tradeoff. Simple projection always provides a view of the whole space (or half of the space, when looking in a given direction) but the view is complex and difficult to interpret. The retina and viewpoint view shows only a small part of a large space, at any moment, but the views are always simple.

The program 4Dviewer can be used to explore this retina and viewpoint scheme, to visualize the dynamics of three-dimensional structures. That is, the examples allow you to explore four-dimensional structures in which time is represented as a fourth spatial dimension. Buttons allow you to move the viewing apparatus around, so as to see different portions of the space. For example, there are buttons for moving the view apparatus in time, so that the situation at different times can be seen. When this is done with the retina and viewpoint aligned with the ordinary spatial axes, as they are when the program starts, this corresponds to a simple animation, with these buttons being used to step forward or backwards among the frames of the animation.

More interesting views can be obtained by moving the viewing apparatus so that one is able to see onto the time axis. Thus, by rotating the retina and viewpoint one can obtains a view in which the time axis extends horizontally from left to right, so that one can see how the structure is changing with time, in a single view. There's a shortcut button to this, labeled "YW plane along Z."

The program allows you to view a few sample objects, selected using buttons. For example, one shows a block with a hole in it that grows and shrinks in a periodic pattern. One can see this happen, using the buttons that change the W coordinate, but perhaps the precise pattern of the growing and shrinking is not apparent. By rotating the viewing apparatus using the shortcut button one can see the pattern of change laid out clearly in space, revealing it to be a sinusoid, and not, for example, a sawtooth (see Figure 9.3a).

Another example shows a caricature of a segment of geologic history. Using the buttons that change the W coordinate one can explore the frames and see how two volcanos grow and erode away. Viewing the scene in a rotated view one sees the dynamics displayed spatially, making it clear (for example) that the growth process is more rapid than the erosion process (see Figure 9.3b). The view shown has the Y axis vertical, as usual, but the W axis, not the X axis, runs from left to right. If we think of W as time, the elevations on the left are earlier than those to the right. We can see the lighter colored volcano, growing, then shrinking, and then being overtaken by the darker one, as that one grows.

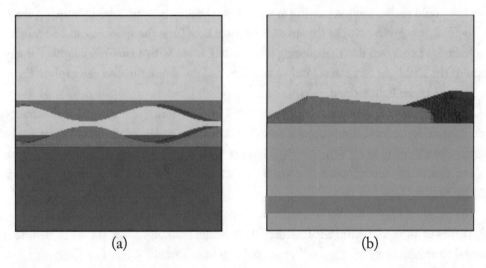

(a)   (b)

Figure 9.3: Displays with time running horizontally: (a) block with varying hole; and (b) two volcanos that grow and then erode away.

The program also allows you to explore a four-dimensional cube, called a *hypercube*, that has colored slabs on each of its faces. It has 24 of these, but groups of 4 faces are colored the same, so you'll only see 6 colors. When you first view it, it will look nothing like a cube. If you increase W a bit, using the button, it'll look more familiar.

The program lets you change your view of things in many different ways. The "arc" buttons let you move the viewing apparatus in a given direction, and automatically rotates the apparatus so it always points to the middle of the space (this is a camera movement called an arc by cinema people.) Or you can move the viewing apparatus around without rotating, corresponding to a *pan* with a camera. And you can rotate the camera in many different ways, since there are a lot of planes in the space in which you can rotate things. As you play with these operations, you'll see strange things happening, including whatever you are looking at disappearing altogether. Remember the flashlight analogy: when that happens, the thing you are looking at just isn't in the part of the space that your viewing apparatus can pick up. If you move the viewing apparatus back, the object will reappear. You'll also see *parts* of things, for the same reason. Even though all the colored slabs in the hypercube are squares, they'll sometimes look like triangles, or other shapes, because only parts of them are in view for a given position of the viewing apparatus.

You'll notice that things are often jagged looking. This results from the way the viewing apparatus is implemented in the program. The program steps along each ray, checking to see if it hits anything. The steps aren't very fine, and when the rays lie along a slanted face the result can be rough.

A good exercise for exploring the hypercube is to try to see the blue, white, and orange faces as squares. You'll probably find that the rotation buttons are your best bet for this, but you'll pass through some odd forms on your way. It's a strange space.

Can this way of viewing a higher-dimensional space support intuition about what these spaces are like? Here's an exploration of this matter.

As a boy I heard that Albert Einstein was the smartest person in the world. He was so smart that he could eat an orange without breaking the skin. This seemed like an excellent demonstration of brilliance: I couldn't even conceive of how this might be done. It seemed definitively impossible. Much later I realized that what I probably heard was a garbled version of some account of Einstein's work with four-dimensional space. There the act is conceptually not hard to perform: one moves the interior of the orange along the fourth dimension, while leaving the peel in place. This can be done without any of the points in the interior intersecting any points in the peel. And of course once the interior is outside the peel one can eat it.

Can one use the retina and viewpoint apparatus to get an informative view of this process? Using only four dimensions, with one being time, requires violating the familiar coherence of objects. In particular, moving the interior of the orange in time so that it is offset from the peel involves unrealistic dynamics. A somewhat more intuitive view results if we work in five dimensions, so that we have four spatial dimensions in addition to time. Now moving the parts of the orange in space can be done without creating anomalous temporal relations.

The retina and viewpoint apparatus can readily be extended to more than four dimensions. As discussed earlier, what is seen is always a three-dimensional portion of the space, no matter how big the space is. The controls needed, however, become more complex, since there are more ways to move the visual apparatus.

The program 5Danimate shows the scenario of the orange. The interior of the orange, and the peel, exist for all values of the time coordinates. Both begin as sets of points in three spatial dimensions, as expected, with coordinates of 0 on the fourth spatial axis, W. As Einstein moves the interior of the orange along this axis, this W coordinate grows for the points in the interior. Now the peel and the interior are spatially separate. In fact, Einstein can now move the interior over, along the X axis, and then move it back along the W axis, so that it ends up next to the peel, on the outside. He can then eat it whenever he wants.

Running the program by pressing the "start" button shows these developments, in an animation in which the movement of time (here the fifth coordinate) is done for you. After you press the start button, time goes back and forth, repeatedly, until you press stop. The interior of the orange moves away along the W coordinate, then to the side along the X coordinate, and back along the W coordinate, to sit next to the peel. Then it reverses course, and repeats.

The action is shown from two different positions of the viewing apparatus. At the beginning and end you see the world along the Z coordinate, with the X and Y coordinate running from left to right, and down to up, as you are used to. At the start you just see the orange peel, because the interior is hidden from view, as usual, and at the end of the cycle you see the interior of the orange sitting next to the peel.

In between you see the action from a different perspective, in which the viewing apparatus has the W axis in view. From this point of view the peel and the interior look like disks, rather than balls, because they aren't very thick along the W axis (see Figure 9.4). In fact, the orange peel is completely open, viewed this way, because if doesn't contain any points with W coordinates that would get in the way of our view. The view makes clear how easy it is for Einstein to remove the interior of the orange in this way. You can decide whether the program gives you any improved understanding of Einstein's incredible feat.

The same program allows you to view another, similar, scenario, by selecting a different scene with a button. Here there's a sealed safe (in three dimensions) containing a gold bar. Exactly the same moves as for the orange serve to take the gold bar out of the safe, and put it back next to the safe. The same viewing positions are used, so you can see that, like the orange, a three-dimensional safe is wide open in four dimensions.

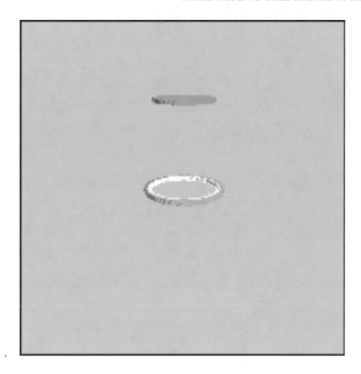

Figure 9.4: Interior of orange (top) separated from peel (bottom).

9.1   APPLYING THE RAMAN PRINCIPLE?

Here we've been presenting various dynamic structures visually. Could we do it non-visually? The Raman principle says yes, if we work out what it is about the spatial structures that people want to know about. Considering Einstein's orange as an example, if we are content with a canned presentation, we could provide a spoken narrative that describes the position of the coordinate axes in the current view, and the position and orientation of the circle, disk, or ring that represents the interior of the orange, and the peel.

Allowing free manipulation of the retina and viewpoint would be more challenging, since one could not work out ahead of time what forms would be seen. The machine vision approach being pioneered by the Bootstrap project (Chapter 6) could be applied to analyze the structure that's created at a given moment, and provide a description of it.

CHAPTER   10

The Aesthetic Potential of Representations of Algorithms

Frieder Nake, a pioneer of computer art, a practicing artist as well as scholar of the subject, has written,

> *Each and every individual piece of algorithmic art is no more than only one instance of the potentially infinitely many from the class of works defined by the algorithm. The tragedy is that the algorithm itself does not often show visual qualities. Its qualities are the potential to generate visual works. But each of its visual products is a shadow only of the algorithm. It is one of its traces, a left-over, a consolation for those who need to see rather than think. If you want to find the masterpiece, you must compare algorithms.*

–Nake, 2010; emphasis added

Indeed, algorithms today are generally represented as program text, and program text, or any text, hardly seems to have visual qualities, or, at least, visual qualities that relate to its meaning.

Text itself does have visual qualities. Typography has a refined aesthetic. And one can use different fonts, or indenting, or unusual arrangements of lines, to convey something visually, as can be seen dramatically in the work of poet Steve McCaffery (do a Google image search to see examples.) But can the text of a program convey the aesthetic potential of what the program does?

What about the visual languages we've discussed in the earlier chapters? They help to highlight a more general issue: very little of the meaning of a visual program is expressed in its visual form, separate from other knowledge that has to be brought to bear, often by reference to textual tags or labels. For example, a block in a blocks language that makes something move can't be understood to do that by observing its shape or color alone; one must read its label. A block that moves is the same shape and color as a block that turns. Similarly, in a dataflow language, without the labels on the operators and connectors, one can have little idea what is going on. Some small part of the structure of the program is available by just looking, but not much of the program's meaning is accessible without reading.

Why does this distinction matter? I suggest that timing is a consideration. Structures like visual form and melodic contour start revealing themselves quickly, and then emerge and develop smoothly over time. By contrast, very little of the meaning of a text, or a program in today's visual languages, is apparent at first, and develops slowly and with effort.

"Effort" suggests another tension. Appreciating visual or musical form, while it can repay concentrated effort, does not require it. But reading text requires close and focused attention.

Can we conceive of expressions of algorithms whose meaning emerges more quickly and smoothly? Could such expressions avoid Nake's tragedy?

Besides Nake's complaint, another reason to explore these matters comes from the emerging performance art called live coding (Collins et al., 2003; Blackwell and Collins, 2005). Live coders work with programs, in front of audience, to produce music (and often associated lightshow-like graphical effects. It's a canon of the art that the program code must be seen: TOPLAP, an organization devoted to the cultivation of the art, requires in its manifesto, "Code should be seen as well as heard, underlying algorithms viewed as well as their visual outcome" (https://toplap.org/wiki/ManifestoDraft).

The TOPLAP Manifesto also suggests, "It is not necessary for a lay audience to understand the code to appreciate it, much as it is not necessary to know how to play guitar in order to appreciate watching a guitar performance. Live coding may be accompanied by an impressive display of manual dexterity and the glorification of the typing interface."

But for me, as an audience member, the aesthetic experience of the performance is diminished by the inclusion of text, however much of a virtuoso of the typewriter the performer may be. For me there is a mismatch between the way the aesthetic value of the music and accompanying graphics emerge, and the way the meaning of the text is revealed, with mutual interference. Concentrating on reading the text distracts from appreciating the music; following the music distracts from interpreting the text.

An emergent issue here is the lack of connection between the text and the music, or at least the obscurity of the connection. The two are certainly connected, since it is the text, when executed as a program, that produces the music. But the connection is difficult to work out, in the time available to the audience. So the undeniable causal connection between the two forms does not help to combine them into an integrated experience.

This effective disconnect is perhaps parallel to the one that produces Nake's frustration. The way he has to express his algorithms is disconnected from the aesthetic product the algorithms create.

Addressing this disconnect again brings us to the question of what might be done about it. Can we conceive of ways to represent algorithms that are more connected to their effects than text?

Considering some approaches to this problem may help to clarify the challenges involved. The Piet programming language (http://www.dangermouse.net/esoteric/piet.html), an exemplar of the fascinating genre of esoteric programming languages (https://en.wikipedia.org/wiki/Esoteric_programming_language), expresses programs as patterns of colors, which can resemble the works of Piet Mondrian (see Figure 10.1). Contributors have written Piet programs that are quite diverse, as also shown the figure, and one might feel that here we are making progress. No text at all is used in these programs; their meaning is entirely expressed in the pattern of colors.

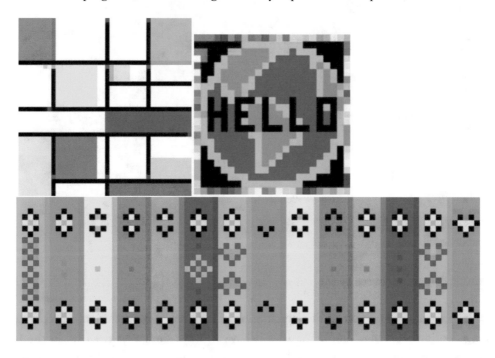

Figure 10.1: Three programs in the Piet language.

However, the aesthetics of Piet programs is diminished by a key fact: while the pattern of colors determines the meaning of the program, the meaning of the program does not determine the pattern of colors. In fact, most of the picture elements in a Piet program have no meaning at all for the program: they are simply ornament. This is a clear instance of the disconnect we seek to eliminate.

Further, the way in which the colored pattern determines the behavior of the program is complex and obscure: an invisible cursor moves about the pattern, turning or not, and changing invisible aspects of the program's state, based on the sequence of colors it traverses. Understanding a Piet program thus requires the kind of detailed study and reasoning that we have stipulated that we want to avoid.

The program Tiles avoids the first of these problems. It produces colored patterns, like those in Figure 10.2, in such a way that its behavior is tied to its appearance; nothing can be changed visually without changing the behavior of the program.

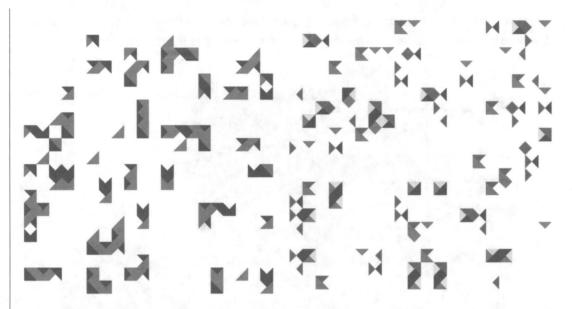

Figure 10.2: Patterns produced by the Times program.

The program is based on an implementation of a model of computation called Wang tiles, or Wang dominoes (Wang, 1965). The tiles behave in ways similar to the tiles in the familiar game of dominoes, except that (a) numbers are replaced by colors, and (b) the tiles have four edges rather than the two ends of dominos. Just as two dominos can be fit together only if the numbers on the touching ends match, so Wang tiles can be fit together only if the colors of the touching edges match.

Wang showed that his tiles are computationally universal, that is, that in principle any computation at all could be expressed by a particular set of tiles. To do this the tiles are colored in such a way that if a row of tiles is formed that represents the starting state of the tape of a Turing machine, an idealized computer, the only way that the tiles can be fit together in the next row will represent the next state of the tape for that Turing machine. The same is true for the next row, and the next, so that the result of running the Turing machine is exactly mirrored in the only possible way of fitting the tiles together.

Note that there is no machinery of any kind hiding behind the scenes here. The coloring of the tiles completely specifies how they can fit together.

The Tiles program does not implement this entire process, and so cannot represent Turing machine computations. While there is only one way that the tiles that represent a Turing machine can be assembled, it can be very tedious to find what that way is. Many tiles will look as if they can fit somewhere, but turn out not to, in that they have to be replaced to allow the tiles to be fit in next to them. So either some smart way of placing the tiles must be used, introducing hidden complexity, or one has to wait indefinitely as tiles are randomly rearranged, looking for a complete fit.

The Tiles program settles for a distant approximation to this: tiles fit together where they can, and may or may not be displaced later to make room for others. It doesn't try to find a complete tiling of the space, as is needed for representing Turing machine computations. (The program starts with a random selection of tile colorings when it begins. But you can change the coloring by clicking on any part of a tile: the color will change, along with that of any tile of the same type, so you can select a set of colorings that you want.)

But putting the difficulties here aside, we can see that tiles does not solve the second problem with Piet: the appearance of a program is related to its behavior in a very complex way. In general it is very hard to say much about the behavior of a collection of tiles, based just on their coloring, just as it is hard to tell what a Piet program will do. Here is our disconnect again.

The program Curves is another example we can consider (see Figure 10.3). It draws on ideas from Truslit's work, discussed in Chapter 8, to produce music from graphical forms. As the program runs, one can change the shape of the curves that the program shows, by dragging the blue dots, and thus change the movement of cursors that travel along the curves. The cursor on the curve to the left generates musical tones, whose pitch is determined by the y coordinate of the cursor. The cursor on the right adds percussion, by generating a beat whenever if passes through an invisible band placed at a specified height.

Figure 10.3: A program that generates sounds from the motion of cursors tracing curves.

This program does better than the previous examples eliminating our problematic disconnect. Its behaviors are easy to see from the form of the program. There are essentially no arbitrary elements in the representation; changing the shape of the curves will change what the program does.

The problem here is *expressiveness*. While Wang tiles can represent any computation, in principle, the curves program can represent only a very narrow range of them, as just described. One would soon tire of the limited possibilities this program offers.

It is possible that extensions of the basic curve tracing idea could expand its expressive potential considerably. For example, the position of the cursor on one curve could change the interpretation of the position of the cursor on another curve. Simple applications of this idea would allow one curve to change what simulated musical instrument is controlled by another curve, or would change at what height the cursor on another curve would produce a beat.

We can put aside thinking about how far one could get in increasing expressiveness along these lines to consider a different kind of example altogether. Listing 10.1 is the text of a program by Frieder Nake, and Figures 10.4 and 10.5 show two outputs from it. This program is an example of the kind of thing Frieder wants to be able to express in his algorithms. It's obvious that the programs tiles and curves are nowhere with respect to this goal.

```
/**********************************

POLYGON HORIZONTAL/VERTICAL
A polygon of n edges, alternatingly horizontal and vertical.
This version 2 has lines of constant color.
Linewidth changes randomly from edge to edge.
The decision for the horizontal to go left is taken in l% of cases.
The decision for the vertical to go up is taken in u% of cases.
The first line to be horizontal or vertical is done at 50/50.
The sketch makes sure that randomly chosen edge-lengths stay inside
the format.
The first and the last vertex are connected by a straight line.


There are 4 cases to distinguish at any given point.
They are controlled by two Boolean variables, vert and dir:
1 vertically up      vert and dir
2 vertically down    vert and not dir
3 horizontally right not vert and dir
4 horizontally left  not vert and not dir
```

```
FN 20 May, 2016
*****************************************/
//GLOBAL PARAMETER SETTINGS
color cBack = color(0); //color of background
color cLine = color(random(0,255),random(0,255),0);
//color of polygon edges, input manually
int wLineLow = 1; //lower limit for random choice of line width of edges
int wLineUp = 7; //upper limit
float l = 50; //percentage of horizontals going left
float u = 50; //percentage of verticals going up
float marg = 50; //margin from image frame to inside
int n = 70; //number of edges in polygon
int fr = 5; //frameRate for display

float x, y, x1, y1; //coordinates of current position and previous one
in polygon
float x0, y0; //coordinates of starting point
float a; //length of next edge in polygon
boolean vert, dir; //control of vert/hor, up/down (resp. right/left)
int count; //number of edges drawn
int wLine; //line width

void setup()
{
size(500, 500); //size of canvas, manually input
background(cBack);
stroke(cLine);
count = 0;
x = random(marg, width-marg); y = random(marg,height-marg); //starting
point
x0 = x; y0 = y; //keep starting point
x1 = x; y1 = y; //previous point reached
vert = (random(1) < 0.5); //initial choice of vertical or horizontal
frameRate(fr);
}
void draw()
```

```
{
if (vert) //go vertically, either up or down
{
dir = random(100) < u; //if dir is true, go up, otherwise down
if (dir)
{ a = random(5, y-marg); y = y-a;} //choose next length, adjust y
else
{ a = random(5, height-marg-y); y = y+a;}
}
else //go horizontally, left or right
{
dir = random(100) < l; //if dir is true, go left, otherwise r
if (dir)
{ a = random(5, x-marg); x = x-a;} //choose next length, adjust x
else
{ a = random(5, width-marg-x); x = x+a;}
}
wLine = int(random(wLineLow, wLineUp)); strokeWeight(wLine);
line(x1, y1, x, y); x1 = x; y1 = y; //draw new edge, save coordinates
vert = !vert; //switch for next polygon edge, alternating direction
count = count + 1; //increase number of finished edges
if (count == n) //check for end
{
line(x, y, x0, y0); //connect last point back to start
saveFrame();
noLoop(); //stop looping and thus the image
}
}
```

Listing 10.1: Program by Frieder Nake.

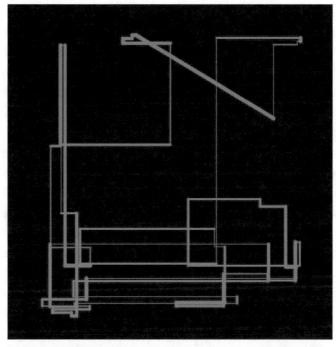

Figure 10.4: Product of Nake program in Listing 10.1.

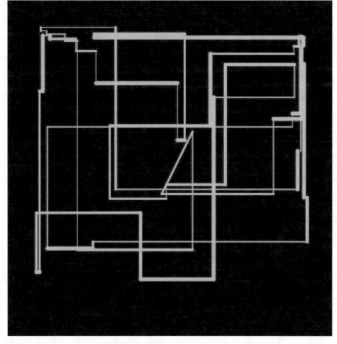

Figure 10.5: Second example of product of Nake program.

Frieder's program is written in Processing, a dialect of the Java programming language, and is a typical textual expression: all details. In fact, Frieder has included some comments to help explain what the program is doing, recognizing that it is too difficult to understand that from the program code itself. Is there any hope of doing something with an example like this?

We can start with a few observations about how Frieder is thinking about what he is doing, based on his comments. He is dealing with lines and their attributes (length, width, color, orientation). He is also dealing with choices, to be made with given probabilities.

Looking through the code, we can also see that there are choices not governed by the given probabilities, but by random selection from ranges, determined by earlier choices. For example, some coordinates are chosen randomly to fall between an earlier chosen coordinate and the edge of the drawing area. It's a corollary to this observation that when Frieder thinks about lines he is thinking about the coordinates of their end points, using Cartesian geometry.

Naively, suppose we ask for an expression of Frieder's algorithm from which it will be apparent that he is producing lines, without have to read and interpret text that refers to lines. We could think about providing program elements that look like lines, and these could have color and width. Because Frieder thinks about coordinates, the lines would also need these: numbers associated in some way with the lines.

We can now think about two challenges. First, how would we express the way in which attributes of the lines are to be selected? We could provide some kind of formula attached to the width attribute of a line, for example, that would specify how the width would be chosen. But using a mathematical formula would not do, because without reading it carefully we could not see what it does. We need some way of expressing dependency that is more transparent. Any ideas?

A second challenge has to do with the *number* of lines in the figure. If there are 50 lines would the program have to contain 50 of these line things? Frieder's Processing program doesn't contain *any* lines: it just contains code that *makes* 50 lines (or whatever number he asks for; he can change that very easily). How could we represent a generic line, and the way its attributes are determined, in a way that makes clear what's going on without close reasoning?

Stepping back, we might conclude that these challenges (and many similar ones that we could frame from this example) simply can't be met. Indeed, a group of students, whom Frieder and I invited to brainstorm the broad challenge of increasing the aesthetic potential of code, mostly concluded that the problem is insoluble. The most constructive suggestions were to stay with the familiar underlying structures of code, and change the presentation of it, as is often done by coloring code, or using indentation, to reveal something about its structure. The students feared the loss of expressive power that seems unavoidable in the alternatives they could think of. We can see that kind of limitation in the Curves program. These students may be right!

But before leaving the question, let's raise the stakes by adding additional motivation for the search. Antranig Basman (2016) has framed a critical contrast between software and other artifacts, noting how very unsatisfactory current software is. For example, he notes that a product of a material craft generally has not only a clearly apparent function, but also a long lifetime, easily in decades and sometimes centuries. Software rarely lasts more than a few years before requiring expensive modification to survive, if it does survive. Basman lists beauty, too, among the desiderata we don't get with software today. But his longer list of contrasts reminds us that there is more at stake than "just" beauty.

So it's worth persisting with the very hard problem that we've encountered here in pursuing Frieder's lament, and the aesthetic challenges in live coding. We can take comfort in the fact that, after all, we've put hardly any time and effort into this problem. We've thought for decades that software is "good enough", as it is, and just lived with it, making minor changes around the edges (for instances of our neglect of innovation, very entertainingly presented, see Bret Victor at http://worrydream.com/#!/TheFutureOfProgramming). From a narrow point of view, of course, it is "good enough." We make it, we use it. But we aren't happy about it, and as Basman suggests, we shouldn't be.

We've seen throughout this book that we have enormous representational resources today, in sound, motion, visual presentation, and interactivity. Perhaps you will find a way to represent a family of lines whose line-ness is manifest, while their number and relationships are determined in a clear way. Why not?

References

Adams, W. K., Paulson, A., and Wieman, C. E. (2008). What levels of guidance promote engaged exploration with interactive simulations? In *AIP Conference Proceedings* (Vol. 1064, No. 1, pp. 59–62). AIP. DOI: 10.1063/1.3021273. 39

Azzopardi, L., Glassey, R., Lalmas, M., Polajnar, T., and Ruthven, I. (2009). PuppyIR: Designing an open source framework for interactive information services for children. In *Proceedings of the Annual Workshop on Human-Computer Interaction and Information Retrieval.* 44

Basman, A., Church, L., Klokmose, C., and Clark, C. (2016). Software and how it lives on-embedding live programs in the world around them. *Proceedings of the Psychology of Programming Interest Group*, Cambridge, UK. 26

Basman, A. (2016). Building software is not [yet] a craft. Proceedings *PPIG Workshop of the Psychology of Programming Interest Group*, Cambridge, UK. Available online at http://www.ppig.org/sites/default/files/2016-PPIG-27th-Basman2.pdf. 84

Benacerraf, P. (1965). What numbers could not be. *The Philosophical Review*, 74(1), 47–73. DOI:: 10.2307/2183530. 34

Blackwell, A. and Collins, N. (2005). The programming language as a musical instrument. Proceedings of *PPIG05 (Psychology of Programming Interest Group)*, 3, 284–289. 76

Bregman, A. (2014). Progress in understanding auditory scene analysis. Recorded discussion at BKN 25 Milestones in Music Cognition, McGill University, July 7–8, 2014. Available at http://www.music.mcgill.ca/bkn25/videos.php#topjump. 56

Brown, J. S. (1984). Discussion at the Workshop on User Centered System Design, Asilomar, CA, December, 1984. 33

Carberry, S., Elzer, S., Green, N., McCoy, K., and Chester, D. (2004). Extending document summarization to information graphics. In *Proceedings of the ACL-04 Workshop: Text Summarization Branches Out* (pp. 3–9). 31

Clark, C. and Basman, A. (2017). Tracing a paradigm for externalization: Avatars and the GPII Nexus. In *Companion to the First International Conference on the Art, Science and Engineering of Programming* (p. 31). ACM. DOI: 10.1145/3079368.3079410. 26

Cleveland, W. S. and McGill, R. (1984). Graphical perception: Theory, experimentation, and application to the development of graphical methods. *Journal of the American Statistical Association*, 79(387), 531–554. DOI: 10.1080/01621459.1984.10478080. 10

Collins, N., McLean, A., Rohrhuber, J., and Ward, A. (2003). Live coding in laptop performance. *Organised Sound*, 8(3), 321–330. DOI: 10.1017/S135577180300030X. 76

Darden, L. (2002). Strategies for discovering mechanisms: Schema instantiation, modular subassembly, forward/backward chaining. *Philosophy of Science*, 69(S3), S354–S365. DOI: 10.1086/341858. 35

diSessa, A., Hammer, D.., Sherin, B., and Kolpakowski, T. (1991). Inventing graphing: Meta-representational expertise in children. *Journal of Mathematical Behavior*, 10(2), 117–160. 13

Eisenberg, M., Basman, A., Hsi, S., and Nickerson, H. (2013). Turtle Temari. In Proceedings of *Bridges 2013: Mathematics, Music, Art, Architecture, Culture* (pp. 255–262). Tessellations Publishing. 55

Fraser, N. (2015). Ten things we've learnt from Blockly. In *Blocks and Beyond Workshop (Blocks and Beyond)*, 2015 IEEE (pp. 49–50). IEEE. DOI: 10.1109/BLOCKS.2015.7369000. 51

Giudice, N. A., Palani, H. P., Brenner, E., and Kramer, K. M. (2012). Learning non-visual graphical information using a touch-based vibro-audio interface. In *Proceedings of the 14th International ACM SIGACCESS Conference on Computers and Accessibility* (pp. 103–110). ACM. DOI: 10.1145/2384916.2384935. 31

Goldin, G. A. and Kaput, J. J. (1996). A joint perspective on the idea of representation in learning and doing mathematics. In Steffe, L. P., Nesher, P., Cobb, P., Goldin, G. A., and Greer, B. (eds.), *Theories of Mathematical Learning. Mahwah*, NJ: Erlbaum, 397–430. 13

Grasshopper image from https://digitalsubstance.files.wordpress.com/2013/01/nudibranch0012e.png.

Hall, V. C. and Kingsley, R. (1968). Conservation and equilibration theory. *The Journal of Genetic Psychology*, 113(2), 195–213. DOI: 10.1080/00221325.1968.10533824. 5

Hamming, R. W. (1980). The Unreasonable Effectiveness of Mathematics. *American Mathematical Monthly*, 87(2), (Feb., 1980), 81–90. DOI: 10.2307/2321982. 4

Hymel, A., Levin, D. T., and Baker, L. J. (2016). Default processing of event sequences. *Journal of Experimental Psychology: Human Perception and Performance*, 42(2), 235. DOI: 10.1037/xhp0000082. 58

Kimura, T. D., Choi, J. W., and Mack, J. M. (1986). A visual language for keyboardless programming. Online at http://openscholarship.wustl.edu/cse_research/841/. 44, 45

Koushik, V. and Lewis, C. (2016a). Work in progress: A non-visual interface for a blocks language. *Proceedings PPIG 2016 Psychology of Programming Annual Conference*, Cambridge, UK, September 7–10, 2016. 49

Koushik, V. and Lewis, C. (2016b). An accessible blocks language: Work in progress. In *Proceedings of the 18th International ACM SIGACCESS Conference on Computers and Accessibility (AS-SETS '16)*. ACM, New York, 317–318. DOI: 10.1145/2982142.2982150. 49

Krantz, D., Luce, D., Suppes, P., and Tversky, A. (2007). Foundations of Measurement. Dover Publications. Lewis, C. (2013). Pushing the Raman principle. In *Proceedings of the 10th International Cross-Disciplinary Conference on Web Accessibility (W4A '13)*. ACM, New York, NY, USA, Article 18, 4 pages. 2

Labview image from http://sine.ni.com/cms/images/casestudies/visteon.jpg?size.

Latour, B. (1986). Visualization and cognition. *Knowledge and Society*, 6(1), 1-40. xiv

Lazzaro, J. (1990). Opening doors for the disabled. *BYTE*, August, 1990. Online at http://codi.tamucc.edu/archives/computing/.lazzaro.htm. 29

Lerner, S., Foster, S. R., and Griswold, W. G. (2015). Polymorphic blocks: Formalism-inspired UI for structured connectors. In *Proceedings of the 33rd Annual ACM Conference on Human Factors in Computing Systems*, (pp. 3063–3072). ACM. DOI: 10.1145/2702123.2702302. 50

Lesh, R. (1981). Applied mathematical problem solving. *Educational Studies in Mathematics*, 12(2), 235–264. DOI: 10.1007/BF00305624. 13

Levin, D. T. and Angelone, B. L. (2008). The visual metacognition questionnaire: A measure of intuitions about vision. *The American Journal of Psychology*, 451–472. DOI: 10.2307/20445476. 58

Levin, D. T., Momen, N., Drivdahl IV, S. B., and Simons, D. J. (2000). Change blindness blindness: The metacognitive error of overestimating change-detection ability. *Visual Cognition*, 7(1-3), 397–412. DOI: 10.1080/135062800394865. 58

Lewis, C. (2013). Pushing the Raman principle. In *Proceedings of the 10th International Cross-Disciplinary Conference on Web Accessibility (W4A '13)*. ACM, New York, Article 18, 4 pages. 43

Lewis, C. (2014). Work in progress report: Non-visual visual programming. In B. duBoulay and J. Good (Eds.) *Proceedings PPIG 2014 Psychology of Programming Annual Conference, 25th Anniversary Event*. Brighton, UK, June 25–27, 2014. 46

Ludi, S. (2015). Position paper: Towards making block- based programming accessible to blind users. *Blocks and Beyond Workshop (Blocks and Beyond)*, 2015 IEEE, Atlanta, GA, pp. 67–69. DOI: 10.1109/BLOCKS.2015.7369005. 51

Machamer, P., Darden, L., and Craver, C. F. (2000). Thinking about mechanisms. *Philosophy of Science*, 67(1), 1–25. DOI: 10.1086/392759. 35

Mackinlay, J. D. (1986). Automating the design of graphical presentations of relational information. *ACM Transactions on Graphics*, 5(2, April), 110–141. DOI: 10.1145/22949.22950. 7, 10

Mackinlay, J. and Genesereth, M. (1985). Expressiveness and language choice. *Data and Knowledge Engineering*, 9(1), 17–29. DOI: 10.1016/0169-023X(85)90025-4. 7

Max image from https://cycling74.com/products/max/.

Millar, S. (1994). *Understanding and Representing Space: Theory and Evidence from Studies with Blind and Sighted Children*. Clarendon Press/Oxford University Press. DOI: 10.1093/acprof: oso/9780198521426.001.0001. 59

Millikan, R. G. (1989). Biosemantics. *The Journal of Philosophy*, 86(6), 281–297. DOI: 10.2307/2027123. 1

Milne, L. R. (2017). Blocks4All: making block programming languages accessible for blind children. *ACM SIGACCESS Accessibility and Computing*, (117), 26–29. DOI: 10.1145/3051519.3051525. 51

Moore, E. and Lewis, C. (2015). Opportunity: Inclusive design for interactive simulations. In *Proceedings of the 17th International ACM SIGACCESS Conference on Computers and Accessibility (ASSETS '15)*. ACM, New York, 395–396. DOI: 10.1145/2700648.2811387. 27

Nake, F. (2010). Paragraphs on computer art, past and present. In *Proceedings of CAT 2010 London Conference* (pp. 55–63). 75

Palmer, S. (1978). Fundamental aspects of cognitive representation. In Rosch, E. and Lloyd, B. (eds.), *Cognition and Categorization*. Lawrence Erlbaum Associates, 259–303. 7, 13

Papert, S. (1971). A computer laboratory for elementary schools. Artificial Intelligence Memo No. 246, LOGO Memo No. 1. MIT Artificial Intelligence Laboratory. Available online at ftp://publications.ai.mit.edu/ai-publications/pdf/AIM-246.pdf. 53

Peirce, C. S. (1878). Illustrations of the logic of science, V. Popular Science Monthly, 13, June 1878. Available at https://en.wikisource.org/wiki/Popular_Science_Monthly/Volume_13/June_1878/Illustrations_of_the_Logic_of_Science_V. 4

Piaget, J. (1971). *Biology and Knowledge*. Chicago: University of Chicago Press. 5

Piaget, J. and Voyat, G. (1979). The possible, the impossible and the necessary. In Murray, F. B. (ed.), *The Impact of Piagetian Theory on Education, Philosophy, Psychiatry and Psychology*, Baltimore: University Park Press, 65–85. 5

Raman, T. V. (1996). Emacspeak–A speech interface. In *Proceedings of the SIGCHI Conference on Human Factors in Computing Systems (CHI '96)*, Tauber, M. J. (ed.). ACM, New York, 66–71. DOI: 10.1145/238386.238405. 33, 43

Raman, T. V. and Gries, D. (1997). Documents mean more than just paper! *Mathematical and Computer Modelling*, 26(1), 45–53. DOI: 10.1016/S0895-7177(97)00103-9. 33, 43

Repp, B. H. (1993a). Music as motion: A synopsis of Alexander Truslit's (1938) Gestaltung und Bewegung in der Musik. *Psychology of Music*, 21(1), 48–72. DOI: 10.1177/030573569302100104. 61, 62

Repp, B. H. (1993b). Musical motion: Some historical and contemporary perspectives. In *Proceedings of the Stockholm Music Acoustics Conference (SMAC)*, (pp. 128–135). Stockholm: Kgl. Musikaliska Akademin. 63

Schwerdtfeger, R. (1991). Making the GUI talk. *BYTE*, December 1991, p. 118–128. 29

Shapiro, R. B., Kelly, A., Ahrens, M., and Fiebrink, R. (2016). *BlockyTalky: A Physical and Distributed Computer Music Toolkit for Kids.* 53

Shepard, R. N. (1964). Circularity in judgments of relative pitch. *The Journal of the Acoustical Society of America*, 36(12), 2346–2353. DOI: 10.1121/1.1919362. 17

Smith, T. L., Lewis, C., and Moore, E. B. (2016a). A Balloon, a sweater, and a wall: Developing design strategies for accessible user experiences with a science simulation. In *International Conference on Universal Access in Human-Computer Interaction*, Springer International Publishing (pp. 147–158). DOI: 10.1007/978-3-319-40238-3_15. 27

Smith, T., Lewis, C., and Moore, E. (2016b). Demonstration: Screen reader support for a complex interactive science simulation. In *Proceedings of the 18th International ACM SIGACCESS Conference on Computers and Accessibility (ASSETS '16)*. ACM, New York, 319–320. DOI: 10.1145/2982142.2982154. 27

Smith, T., Lewis, C., and Moore, E. (2017). Description strategies to make an interactive science simulation accessible. *Journal on Technology and Persons with Disabilities*, 5(22), 225–238. 27

Suchman, L. (2007). *Human-machine Reconfigurations: Plans and Situated Actions*. Cambridge University Press. xiii

Szpiro, S. F. A., Hashash, S., Zhao, Y., and Azenkot, S. (2016). How people with low vision access computing devices: Understanding challenges and opportunities. In *Proceedings of the 18th International ACM SIGACCESS Conference on Computers and Accessibility* (pp. 171–180). ACM. DOI: 10.1145/2982142.2982168. 51

Vasek, M. (2012). Representing expressive types in blocks programming languages. In Honors Thesis Collection, Wellesley College, online at http://repository.wellesley.edu/thesiscollection/24/. 50

Viviani, P. and Cenzato, M. (1985). Segmentation and coupling in complex movements. *The Journal of Experimental Psychology: Human Perception and Performance*, 11(6), 828–45. DOI: 10.1037/0096-1523.11.6.828. 63

Viviani, P. and Schneider, R. (1991). A developmental study of the relationship between geometry and kinematics in drawing movements. *Journal of Experimental Psychology: Human Perception and Performance*, 17(1), 198–218. DOI: 10.1037/0096-1523.17.1.198. 63

Viviani, P. and Terzuolo, C. (1982). Trajectory determines movement dynamics. *Neuroscience*, 7(2), 431–437. DOI: 10.1016/0306-4522(82)90277-9. 63

Walker, B. N. and Mauney, L. M. (2010). Universal design of auditory graphs: A comparison of sonification mappings for visually impaired and sighted listeners. *ACM Transactions on Accessible Computing (TACCESS)*, 2(3), 12. DOI: 10.1145/1714458.1714459. 31

Wang, Hao. (1965). "Games, logic and computers." *Scientific American* 213.5: 98–106. DOI: 10.1038/scientificamerican1165-98. 78

WebAIM (2017). *Designing for Screen Reader Compatibility*. Online at https://webaim.org/techniques/screenreader/. 29

White, T. and Pea, R. (2011). Distributed by design: On the promises and pitfalls of collaborative learning with multiple representations. *Journal of the Learning Sciences*, 20(3), 489–547. DOI: 10.1080/10508406.2010.542700. 13

Wigner, E. P. (1995). The unreasonable effectiveness of mathematics in the natural sciences. *The Collected Works of Eugene Paul Wigner–Part B: Historical, Philosophical and Socio-Political Papers*, 6, 534–549. DOI: 10.1007/978-3-642-78374-6_41. 4

Winer, G. A., Craig, R. K., and Weinbaum, E. (1992). Adults' failure on misleading weight-conservation tests: A developmental analysis. *Developmental Psychology*, 28(1), 109. DOI: 10.1037/0012-1649.28.1.109. 5

Wyman, B., Timpson, C., Gillam, S., and Bahram, S. (2016). Inclusive design: From approach to execution. MW2016: Museums and the Web 2016, *The Annual Conference of Museums and the Web*, Los Angeles, CA. Online at http://mw2016.museumsandtheweb.com/paper/inclusive-design-from-approach-to-execution/. 23

Zetzsche, C., Galbraith, C., Wolter, J., and Schill, K. (2007). Navigation based on a sensorimotor representation: a virtual reality study. In *Human Vision and Electronic Imaging* (p. 64921G). DOI: 10.1117/12.711121. 24, 25

Author Biography

Clayton Lewis is a Professor of Computer Science and Fellow of the Institute of Cognitive Science, at the University of Colorado, Boulder, where he has been based since 1984. He is well known for his research on evaluation methods in user interface design. Two methods to which he and his colleagues have contributed—the thinking aloud method and the cognitive walkthrough—are in regular use in software development organizations around the world. He has also contributed to cognitive assistive technology, to programming language design, to educational technology, and to cognitive theory in causal attribution and learning. He was named University of Colorado President's Teaching Scholar in 1989, a life title signifying the University's highest award for teaching. In Spring 2017 he was a fellow at the Hanse-Wissenschaftskolleg in Delmenhort, Germany.

Lewis earned an AB in mathematics from Princeton University, an MS from MIT, for interdisciplinary study in mathematics and linguistics, and a Ph.D. from the University of Michigan in experimental psychology. He was elected to the ACM CHI Academy in 2009, recognizing his contributions to the field of human-computer interaction. In 2011, he was further recognized by the ACM CHI Social Impact Award for his work on technology for people with cognitive, language, and learning disabilities.

Printed in the United States
by Baker & Taylor Publisher Services